Royal Illuminated Manuscripts
from King Athelstan to Henry VIII

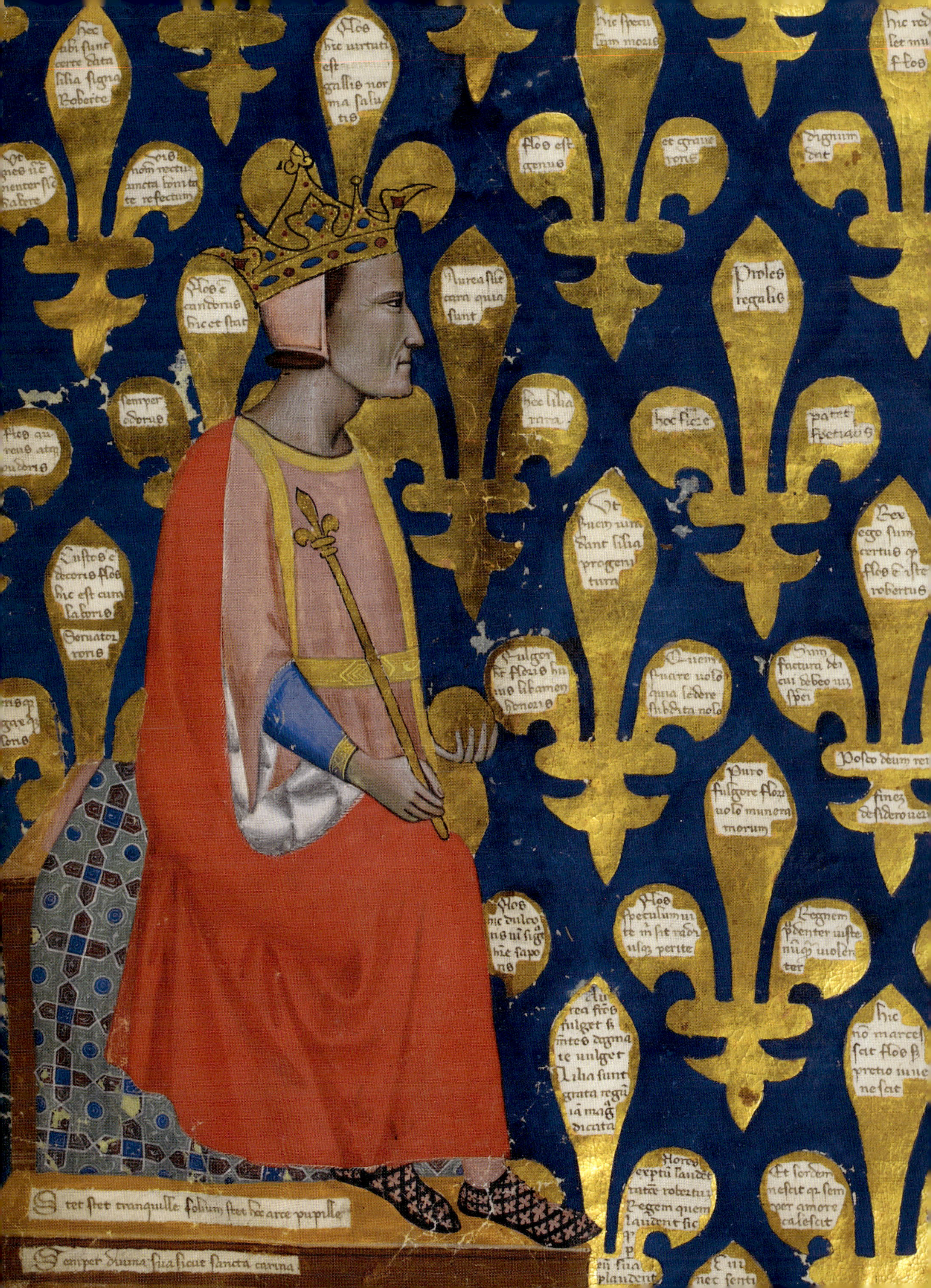

Stet stet tranquille solium stet hec arce pupille
Semper diuina sua sicut sancta carina

Royal Illuminated Manuscripts

from King Athelstan to Henry VIII

Scot McKendrick and Kathleen Doyle

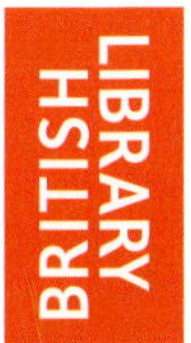

Introduction

Scot McKendrick

Surviving handwritten books associated with successive kings and queens of England form a remarkable inheritance. Together they offer by far the largest body of evidence for the interplay between two critical parts of British cultural heritage: its monarchy and its medieval art. Parts of the built legacy of the British monarchy from the Middle Ages – for example, the White Tower of London, Westminster Abbey and Windsor Castle – have a high profile in national and international public consciousness. Royal manuscripts in contrast have much lower public recognition, concealed from all but scholarly view for centuries in libraries, the very means of their preservation. Yet their survival is a miracle worthy of much greater recognition. Despite centuries of warfare, social, religious and cultural disruption, royal manuscripts still exist in large numbers. Tens of thousands of pages in them bear some of the most outstanding examples of decorative and figurative painting that survive in Britain from between the eighth and sixteenth centuries. The state of preservation of these remarkable illuminations is moreover notably high, their colours often as vivid as when they were first painted and their gold still making their pages glow and flicker in the light for us, as they did for those who first viewed them so many centuries ago. The achievement of the creators of these great works is manifest to this day. As one contemporary inscription puts it, 'The beauty of this book displays my genius.'

Yet royal manuscripts do much more than declare the artistry of their makers. They offer unique insights into the life and aspirations of those for whom they were made. In them we have the most vivid surviving sources for understanding royal identity, moral and religious beliefs, learning and politics. Through careful interpretation of their texts and images, we can deepen our understanding of what it was to be a king in the Middle Ages and find answers to some key questions about medieval monarchs. How, for example, did they relate to the ultimate ruler of all, God, and to his representation on Earth, the Church? What was expected of young princes of the blood, born to power? To whom did they look to inform their conduct as rulers? What knowledge did rulers need, and seek, to enhance their power and authority? How did they shape their multiple identities as dynast, crowned king, law-giver, supreme military commander and pinnacle of the most exclusive and fashionable part of society? How did they give visible expression to their political rivalry with their Continental cousins? Complemented by documentary evidence, royal manuscripts greatly enrich our knowledge of the history of Britain and its monarchy.

Thanks to a generous gift to the nation by George II in 1757, most surviving royal manuscripts are still preserved together as a group. Now held by the British Library and kept as a discrete collection, the Royal manuscripts number nearly two thousand volumes. Together with some nine thousand printed books also donated by George II, they form what has become known as the Old Royal library. Within it are the books inherited by the Hanoverian monarch from his royal predecessors. Subsequently his grandson George III built up his own vast personal library. It too is now held by the British Library and retained as another discrete collection, this time called the King's collection. The collections of books formed by subsequent British monarchs are retained elsewhere, in the Royal Collection held in trust by HRH Queen Elizabeth II for her successors and the British nation, most notably in the Royal Library, Windsor Castle. Of these three English royal libraries the Old Royal library is by far the most significant for its medieval illuminated manuscripts and associations with the monarchs of the Middle Ages.

The present book showcases illuminated manuscripts associated with the English royal family principally through those still forming part of the Old Royal library. Thirty manuscripts have been selected from around 1200 in this collection that are in some way decorated. To complement them we have also chosen eleven volumes that now form parts of other collections in the British Library, but were also once associated with English monarchs. Some of these formerly belonged to the Old Royal library. Such is the wealth of material available within the Royal and other collections of the British Library that we were able to formulate and explore the role of illuminated manuscripts owned by English monarchs in this publication solely from the Library's resources.

The manuscripts we have selected are presented chronologically, starting in the Anglo-Saxon period when the English were first unified under a single king and ending after the Tudor monarch, Henry VIII, had broken with the Church at Rome. Within England alone much changed during this period, often with bloody consequences. Not least, dynasties came and went. The death of Harold at the battle of Hastings in 1066 ended Anglo-Saxon rule, and William of Normandy's victory led to England becoming part of a wider domain that extended across the Channel. Its king then spent most of his life in France. Only after massive territorial losses in France under King John did the perspective of English monarchs begin to change. In the following century Edward III's dynastic claim to the title 'King of France' led to the so-called Hundred Years War between England and France (1335–1453). At the same time, the Black Death decimated the population of England and the rest of Europe. In England civil war raged several times over the centuries, not least during the Wars of the Roses in the second half of the fifteenth century. Successively Lancastrian and Yorkist regimes were brought to an end. Tudor rule brought further change, not least in the religious lives of its subjects.

Outstanding as products and survivors of these turbulent times, illuminated manuscripts help nuance our view of the Middle Ages and of the rulers of England during that period. Through them we can track the evolving interaction of English monarchs and the Christian Church. Although they vary in appearance and use, many, as those presented here, are decorated, some extravagantly so. Several were employed in Christian worship, while others were perused by individuals in the course of their devotions. Most prominent are lavish copies of the Psalms and the Gospels (1, 3, 5, 8, 12, 18, 41), and the late medieval bestseller, the Book of Hours

(22, 24). Some of these volumes were gifts from monarchs (2, 4), whereas others were gifts to them (8, 25, 26). Yet others were books commissioned by royalty for their own use (14, 41). All bear witness to the centrality of Christian religion and the Church in the lives of English monarchs and the importance of English royalty in the creation of richly ornamented and illustrated copies of Christian and Church texts.

As well as enabling us to track such a major aspect of the lives of successive monarchs over several centuries, illuminated manuscripts can provide telling insights about specific English monarchs. Generally regarded as the foundations of the Old Royal library, the deluxe manuscripts collected by Edward IV offer a distinctive means of understanding why his court was considered by one European visitor as 'the most splendid court … in all Christendom' – and this after he had just experienced the renowned wonders of the court of the duke of Burgundy. Homogenous in their lavish outward appearance, Edward's manuscripts were produced by highly accomplished commercial scribes and illuminators in one of the most important centres of painting and the other arts in the late Middle Ages, the Flemish town of Bruges (30–33). In artistic style and textual content they reflect the King's preference for what was fashionable at the court of his brother-in-law, Charles the Bold, Duke of Burgundy (d. 1477). They also provide vivid evidence of the reading matter and imagery which during a period of considerable prosperity Edward and his court drew on both to be entertained and to learn from the experience of past rulers and their subjects.

Widening the viewpoint again we find that illuminated manuscripts can help inform us on the ways in which books contributed to the shaping of young royal princes and offered mature royalty models on which to base their lives and actions. Some texts that they read in their early years drew on the Aristotelian idea that to rule successfully, a prince should first learn how to govern himself. Known as 'Mirrors of Princes', these texts stressed the importance of Christian values and chivalric virtues in the upbringing of a future king (17, 21). Copies of them made for the personal use of young princes and their tutors embellished their appearance and meaning with rich decoration and illustrations. Because knowledge of history was also recommended as engendering wisdom, virtue and knightly conduct, royalty also read a wide range of historical and legendary texts featuring heroes and heroines from the Bible, Christian hagiography, ancient mythology and Greek and Roman history and legend. Several heroes from the past gained special esteem as models to emulate: Solomon for his wisdom (20), Alexander and Caesar for their military accomplishments (23, 29, 31) and Hercules for his chivalric virtues. One further model of kingship from the Old Testament was the complex figure of King David, the supposed author of the Psalms (5, 8, 41). Rich narrative and iconic imagery was developed around these models of power from the past and continually reinterpreted for succeeding rulers and their families. Parallel, but distinctively different models were developed for the education of female members of royalty (28).

Manuscripts from the Old Royal library also help us understand the knowledge world of medieval monarchs. Works of princely instruction repeatedly stressed the importance of the intellectual formation of kings and encouraged an appetite for knowledge. Handwritten books were the principal means by which knowledge was transmitted before the advent of printing with movable type in the middle of the fifteenth century. Surviving manuscripts track English royal engagement with an evolving corpus of texts, the authors of which built on the learning of classical Greece and Rome and developed their own distinctive contribution to western European thought. These books were intended for, presented to or appropriated by English kings as books of reference and learning. While some attest to monastic scholarly interests and came into royal possession only in the early modern period, others reflect the types of texts and cycles of illustrations that transmitted knowledge considered particularly valuable for a king or provided handy digests of information about the natural and spiritual world for a busy monarch (35).

Illuminated manuscripts also contributed to the complex nexus of identities developed by English monarchs. They aided men to present and understand their identity as monarchs, distinct from other men through genealogical descent and formal coronation, and through their roles as supreme law-giver, military leader and arbiter of chivalric conduct and courtly taste. They did so in lavishly illustrated genealogies (10), accounts of coronations (15), books of legal statutes, military treatises (9) and records of the chivalric Order of the Garter founded by Edward III. The 'fashionable exclusivity' of English royalty was compounded by their persistent engagement with French rather than English literary texts well beyond the adoption of English within England in most other social and cultural contexts.

These royal books also enrich our understanding of the relationship between English royalty and their Continental counterparts. Many of the most beautiful manuscripts acquired by English monarchs during the late medieval period were of Continental rather than English origin. Through them we observe both the close affinity of English royalty with fashionable Continental styles and their efforts at appropriation of the art and culture of their longstanding political rival, France. Together with contemporary documents, surviving manuscripts provide important insights into the cultural life of the English monarch and his family and its relationship to that of their blood relations on the Continent. In them we catch glimpses of books as diplomatic and courtly gifts (29, 37), symbols of military and political ascendancy (14), unique remnants of the personal worlds of successive French brides of English kings (26), objects of the commercial trade in luxury goods, and evidence of evolving English royal ambition and taste.

The forty-seven plates in this book provide vivid and unique insights into a world very different from our own. They also include some of the finest painting to survive from the Middle Ages, painstakingly created over lengthy periods by the leading artists of their day. Although we know so much less about them than the royalty who came to own their works (indeed, most will continue to be anonymous, their biographies beyond our grasp after the passage of so many centuries), what remains – their beautiful illustrations, decoration and script – is a monument to their creativity and skill. This volume seeks to make them better known, their significance better understood and their future secure for many more centuries.

1 A manumission by King Athelstan

This extraordinary book is one of the earliest survivals from the Old Royal library. It contains the Four Gospels, and was probably copied from the same exemplar as that of its more famous relation, the Lindisfarne Gospels. It may have been made at the monastery on the tidal island of Lindisfarne, or Holy Island, in Northumbria.

Pictured here is the end of the genealogy of Christ in Mathew (1:16–17), with large initial letters at the beginning of verse 18, made up of colourful intertwined birds' heads. The first word of this verse (*Christi*) often received special decoration because it is the first mention of Christ's name. The letters making up the first two words are set out in 'display script' to emphasise their importance and, as was typical in Anglo-Saxon illuminated copies, Christ's name itself is abbreviated and written in Greek, not Latin, characters. While this should take the form of a Chi (shaped like an 'X'), a Rho ('P') and an Iota ('I'), this scribe erroneously shaped the Rho like an 'n'.

In the early part of the ninth century, the space at the end of the first column was used to record King Athelstan's (r. 924–939) freeing or manumission of the slave Eadhelm. The earliest surviving English manumission, this is also a very early example of the practice of inserting important records into sacred books (compare no. 3). This account was written in Old English, and records that 'King Athelstan freed Eadhelm straight away, as soon as he became king' in the presence of witnesses, and sworn on the King's *haligdom*, or holy relics. Other additions to the book, such as musical notation, together with its discolouration indicate that the manuscript continued to be used as a service book for centuries after its production.

An Insular Gospel Book
Northumbria (Lindisfarne?), first half of the 8th century
280 x 220 mm
British Library, Royal 1 B. vii, f. 15v

cob autem genuit ioseph
uirum mariæ de qua na
tus est ihs qui uocatur xps
Omnes autem ergo gene
rationes
Ab abraham usque ad da
uid generationes
quattuordecim
A dauid usque ad trans
migrationem ba
bilonis generationes
quattuordecim
A transmigrationem
babilonis usque ad xpm
generationes
quattuordecim

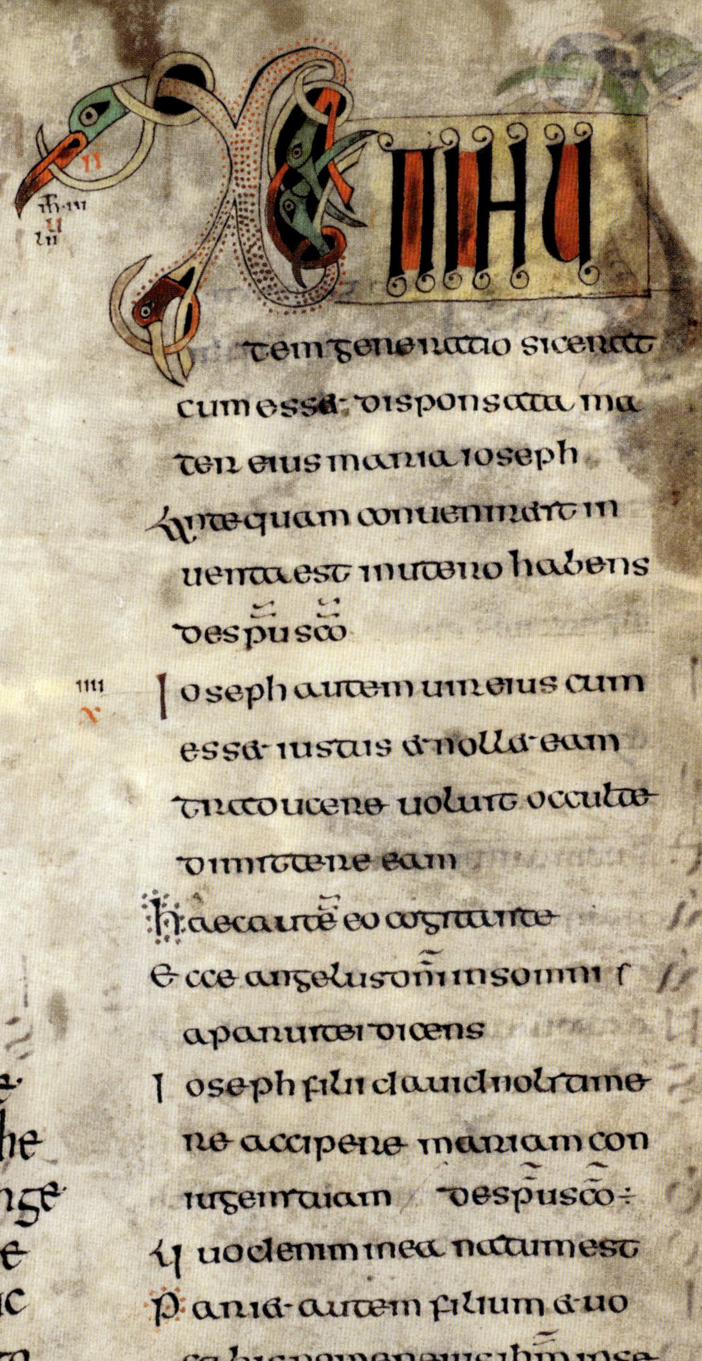

XPI autem generatio sic erat
cum esset disponsata ma
ter eius maria ioseph
antequam convenirent in
uenta est in utero habens
de spu sco
Ioseph autem uir eius cum
esset iustus & nollet eam
traducere uoluit occulte
dimittere eam
Haec autem eo cogitante
ecce angelus dni in somnis
apparuit ei dicens
Ioseph fili dauid noli time
re accipere mariam con
iugem tuam de spu sco
quod enim in ea natum est
pariet autem filium & uo
cabis nomen eius ihm ipse
enim saluum faciet populum
suum a peccatis eorum
hoc autem totum factum est
ut adimpleretur id quod
dictum est a dno per prophe
tam dicens

Æðelstan cyng gefreode
Eadelm forraðe þæs ðe he
ærest cyng wæs. þæt wæs on ge
wytnesse ælfheah masse
preost & se hired & ælfric
se gerefa & þurnoð hwita
& eanstan wrafost & byrnn
stan massepreost. se þe
ðæt on þrinde hæbbe he godes
un miltse & ealler ðær halig
domes ðe ic on angel cynn
begeat mid godes miltse
þican ðan bearnan þæ hilcan
ðær ic þan fædan an :~

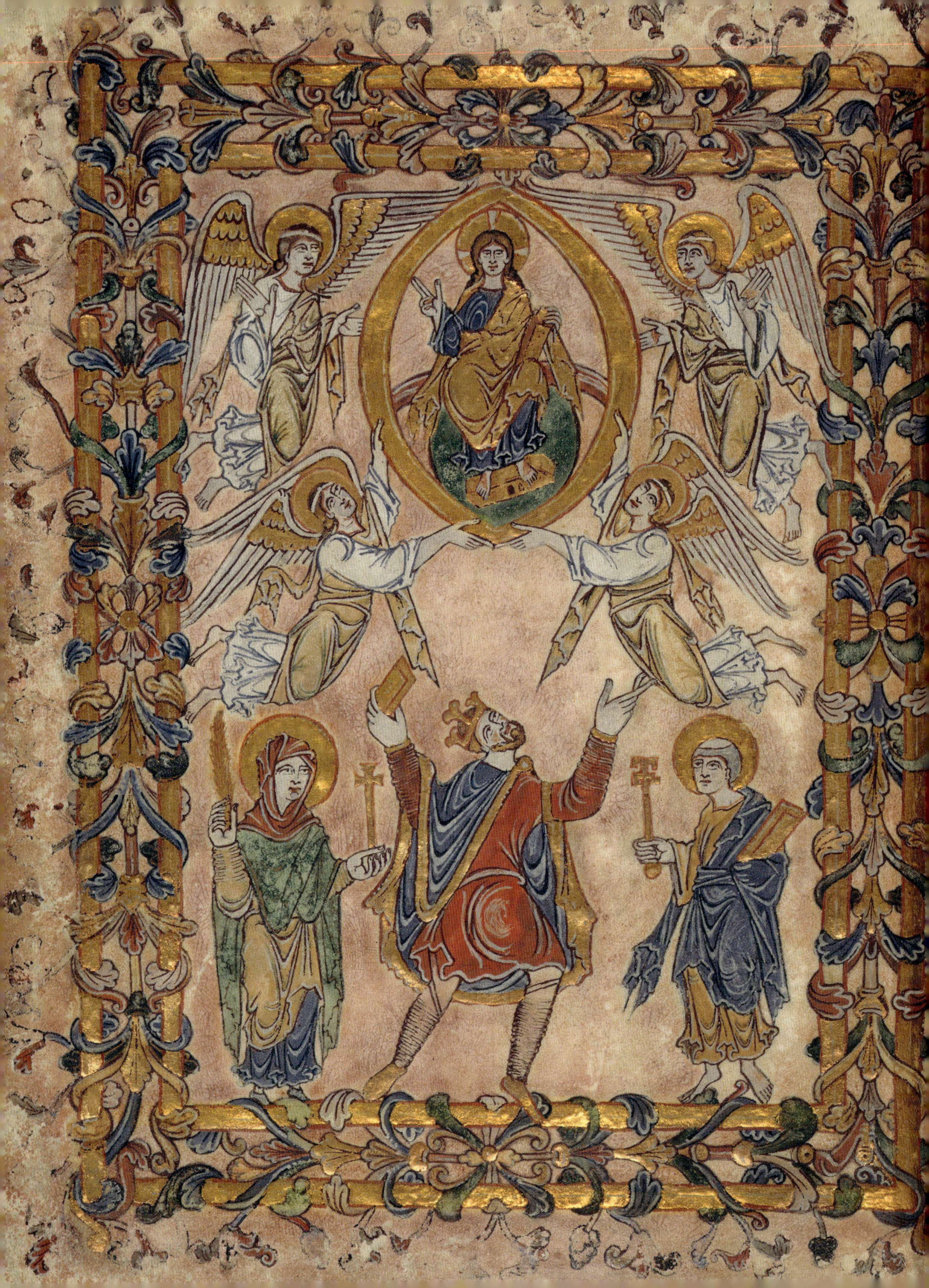

2 King Edgar and Christ in majesty

King Edgar (d. 975), king of all of England from 959, was a reformer whose bishops imposed the Benedictine rule on monastic communities, such as the one at New Minster, Winchester. This charter, in the unusual format of a book rather than a single sheet of parchment, commemorates the introduction of the Rule at New Minster in 964. The manuscript was completed two years later, and is written entirely in gold – the only known late Anglo-Saxon example. Its importance is further emphasised by the large full-page image of the King at the beginning of the book.

In the painting, surrounded by a typically lavish Anglo-Saxon border, Edgar holds a book, presumably this very book. He offers it to Christ above, who is seated on a rainbow in glory, being held aloft by angels. Flanking Edgar are the two patron saints of the abbey, the Virgin Mary and St Peter (who are also pictured with King Cnut and Queen Emma in the Winchester *Liber vitae* [no. 4]. The King's relationship to Christ is made explicit by an inscription on the page facing the image: 'Thus he who established the stars sits on a lofty throne. King Edgar, prostrate and venerating, adores him.' Through its text, decoration and imagery, the book illustrates the importance of the King's patronage, but also the limitations of his power.

The New Minster Charter
Winchester, 966
225 x 165 mm
British Library, Cotton Vespasian A. viii, f. 2v

3 The beginning of Mark

From an early period, books containing only the Four Gospels were amongst the
most common of biblical texts. Many deluxe copies feature elaborate full-page
decoration at the beginning of each Gospel, often, as here, illuminated with gold.
This elegant copy also has gold initials at the beginning of each biblical verse.
The border surrounding the beginning of Mark features lush stylised leaves
characteristic of late Anglo-Saxon decoration (compare no. 2), with embedded
roundels of saints. The saint on the right holds a golden book, perhaps analogous
to the type of jewelled or precious cover that might originally have been affixed
to this copy of the Gospels.

The manuscript belonged to Christ Church, Canterbury, and may have been made
there. It is now known as the Cnut Gospels because of an added text in Old
English that names Cnut, King of England (r. 1016–35) and his brother Harold as
'brothers' of the monastery. On the page opposite the beginning of Mark's Gospel
another inscription confirmed the religious community's liberties, also naming the
King. Perhaps Cnut paid for this deluxe copy of the Gospels and presented it to
the community: the first inscription is written as if Cnut was speaking: 'I myself
took the charters … and laid them on Christ's own altar.' However, there is no
mention of a donation of this book, which might be expected if it was a gift from
the King.

This manuscript entered the Old Royal library only at the beginning of the
seventeenth century, when Henry Frederick, Prince of Wales (d. 1612), the eldest
son of James I acquired the library of John, 1st Baron Lumley (b. *c.* 1533, d. 1609).

The Cnut Gospels
Southern England, early 11th century (before 1017–1020)
350 x 270 mm
British Library, Royal 1 D. ix, f. 45

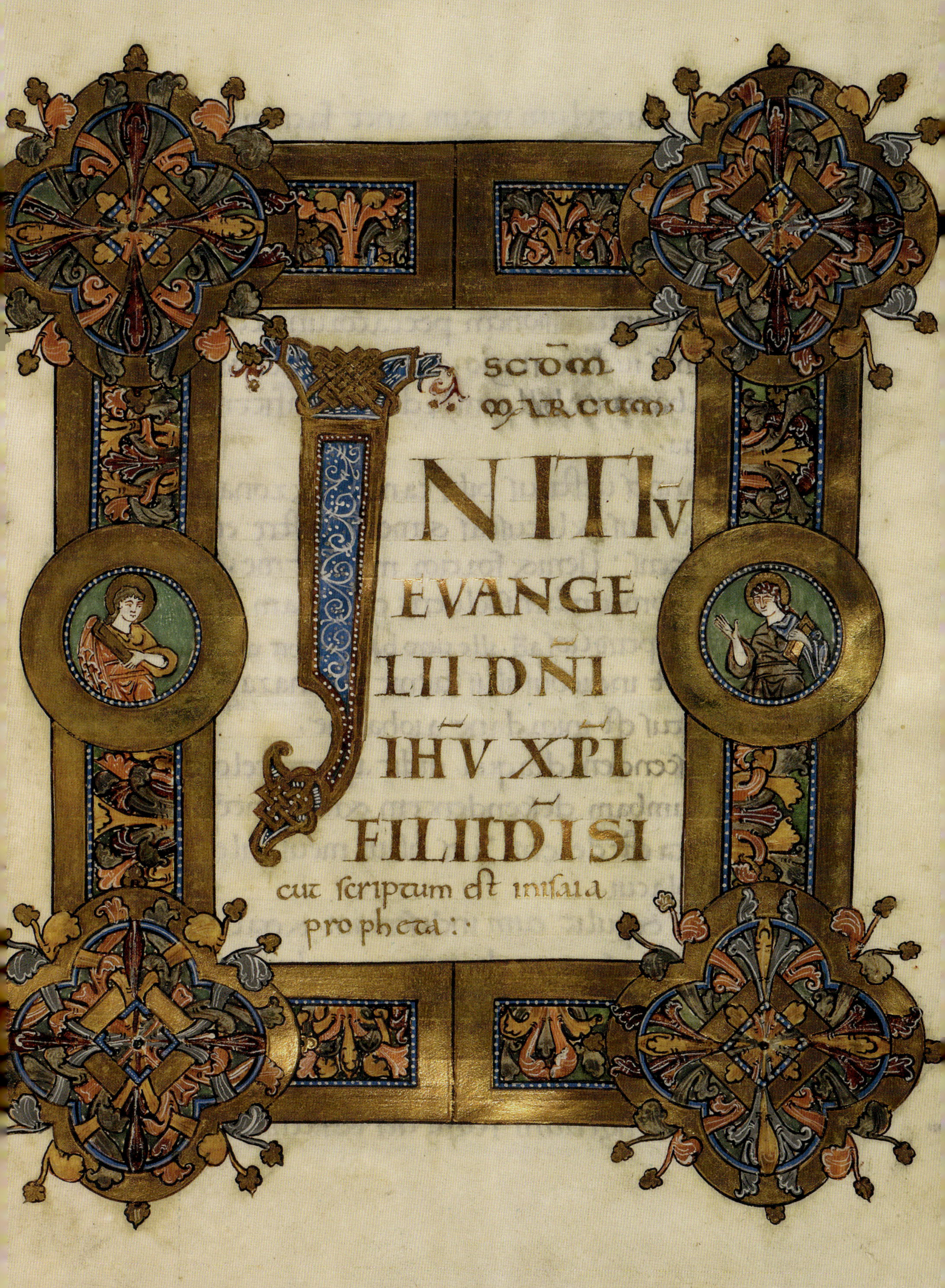

SCDM
MARCUM
INITIV
EVANGE
LII DNI
IHV XPI
FILII DI SI
cui scriptum est in isaia
propheta :·

4 A donation of King Cnut and Queen Emma to New Minster

The image at the beginning of this book is a record of a real event: King Cnut (d. 1035) and his queen Emma of Normandy (d. 1052), the widow of Ethelred the Unready, presenting a cross to the church of New Minster, Winchester. The cross itself no longer survives, but this near-contemporary account of its gift remains. However, the picture includes more than the royal donors – the couple are presented in their place in the spiritual as well as the temporal world. Above the King and Queen are the patron saints of New Minster, the Virgin Mary and St Peter, the latter with his identifying attribute of the keys of heaven. Between them, angels present Emma with a veil and Cnut with a crown. The central figure of the image is the risen Christ, directly above the cross, holding an open book.

The earthly hierarchy is also depicted: below the King and Queen are the monks of New Minster. The central monk also grasps an open book, probably this book itself, a book of life (*Liber vitae*), so-called because it includes in it a list of the monks of the community, so that 'by making a record on earth in written form, [those named] may be inscribed into the pages of the heavenly'. The first inscribed names are those of the King and Queen themselves. Their identities are also made clear by the inscription of their names next to their portraits: 'Ælfgifu regina' (Queen Emma) and 'Cnut rex' (King Cnut).

The New Minster *Liber Vitae*
Winchester (New Minster), 1031
255 x 150 mm
British Library, Stowe 944, f. 6

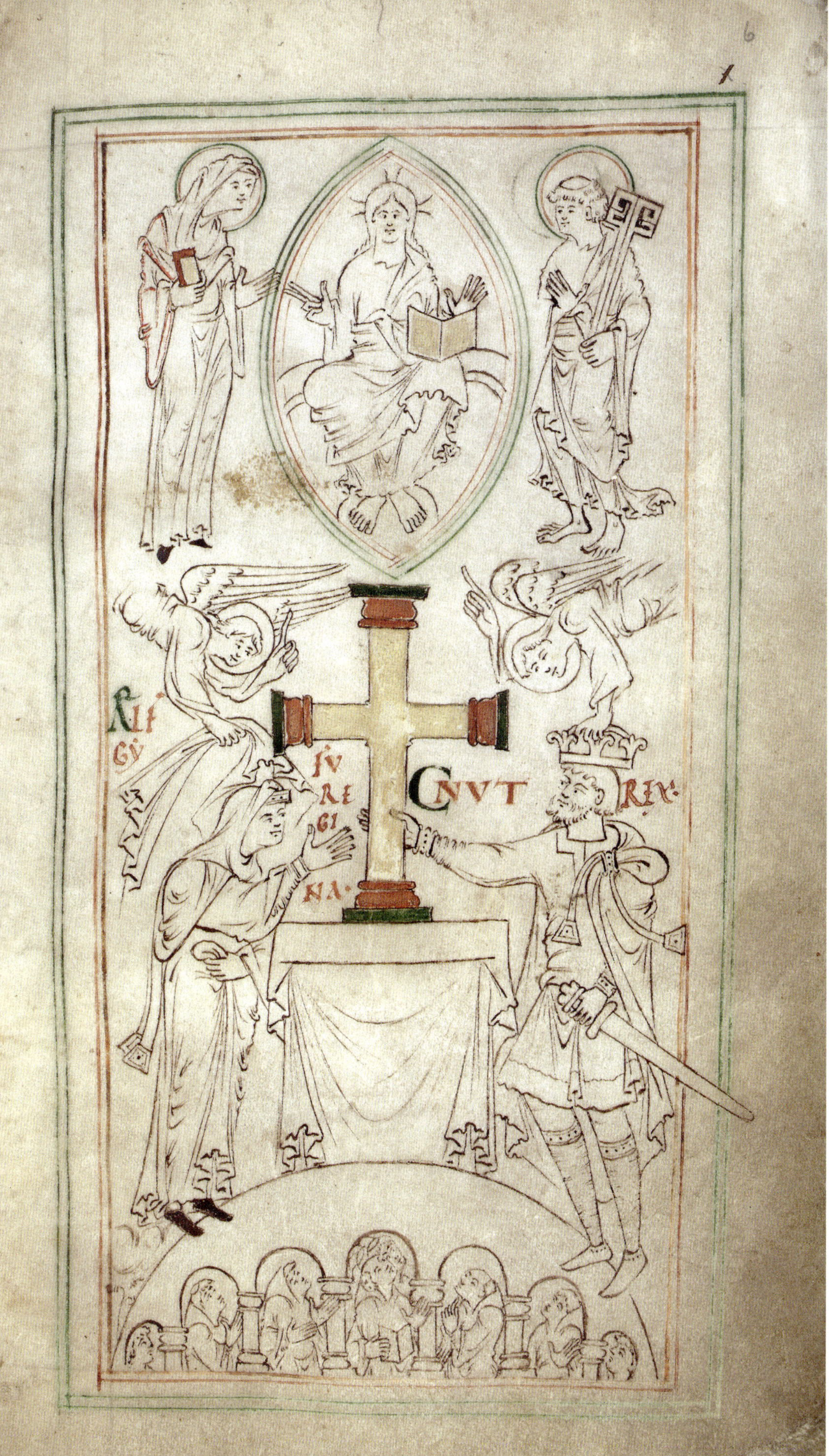
ÆLF
GY
VA
IV
RE
GI
NA
CNVT
REX

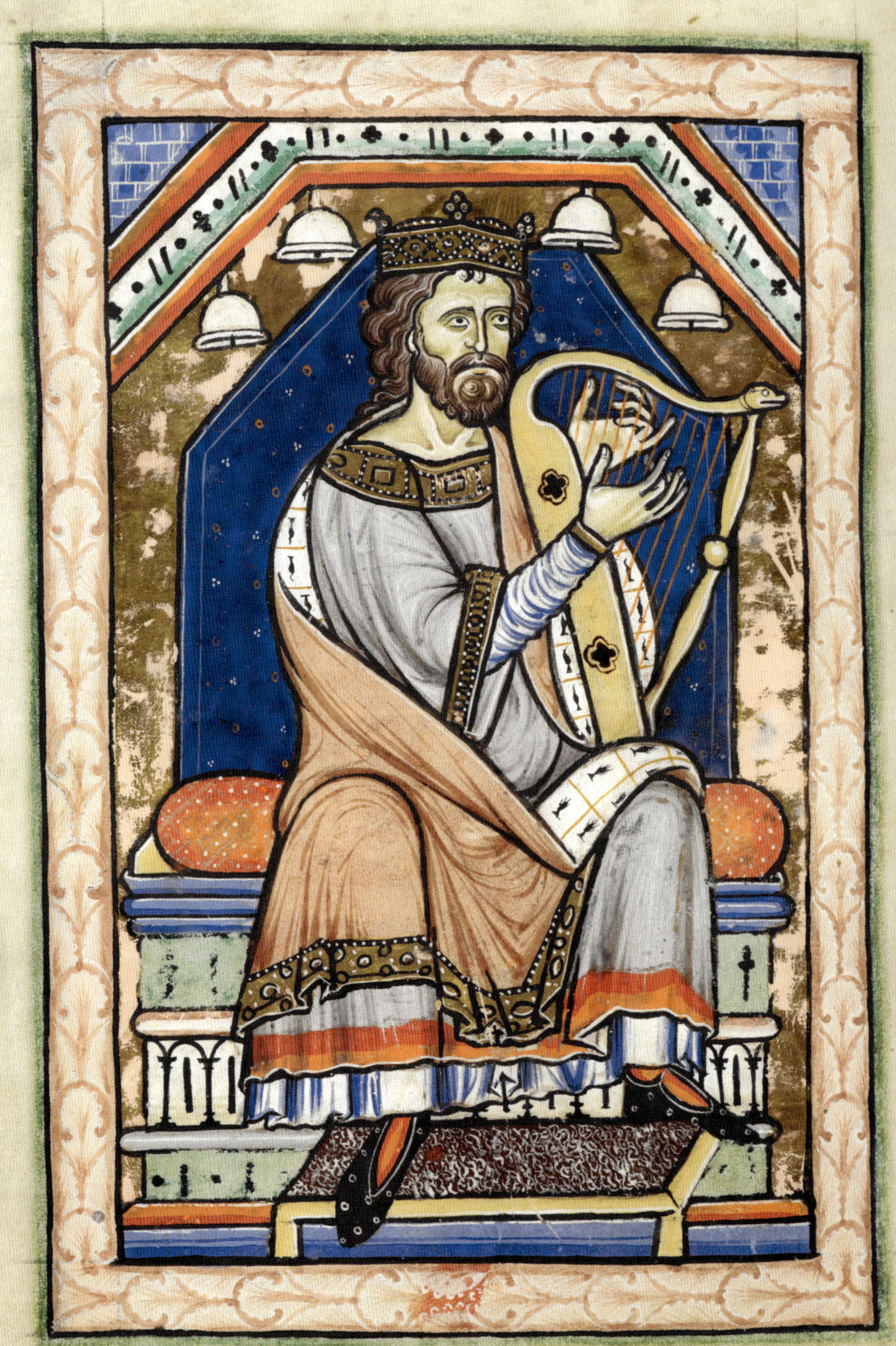

5 King David as musician

From an early period the Psalms formed the basis for monastic services as well as private devotion. Volumes containing only the Psalms without other biblical books, accompanied by calendars with saints' days and other devotional material, are known as Psalters. Psalters are amongst the most numerous manuscripts of any kind to survive from the medieval period.

Many Psalms are described as Psalms 'of David', and accordingly decorated Psalters typically include images of significant events in his life. The most common illustration to the beginning of the Psalms is an image of David as king and musician holding a harp, indicating both his authorship and the nature of Psalms as songs.

This image is present in the famous Westminster Psalter, so-called because it is associated with Westminster Abbey. The lavish volume may have been commissioned by one of its abbots at the beginning of the thirteenth century, to judge by the style of its decoration, which constitutes some of the most elegant and refined painting of the period. The names of their artists are not known, but the painter responsible for the figure of King David was probably an itinerant layman rather than a monk. Prayers added in the fourteenth and fifteenth centuries and a reference to the Psalter in a fourteenth-century inventory attest to its continued use at the Abbey.

The Westminster Psalter
London, c. 1200
230 x 155 mm
British Library, Royal 2 A. xxii, f. 14v

6 The king of beasts

Bestiaries, or books of beasts, contained information about animals from a variety of ancient sources such as the *Naturalis historia* of Pliny the elder (d. 79), the *Historia animalium* of Aristotle (d. 322 BC), and an anonymous Greek compilation called the *Physiologus* (the Naturalist). Passages from the *Etymologiae* of Isidore of Seville (d. 636), which itself drew upon the *Hexaemeron* of St Ambrose (d. 399), were combined with these various extracts to form a compendium of etymology, natural history, and most importantly, allegory or moralisations to be drawn from animal behaviour. The number and types of animals included in bestiaries varied, but many copies start with a description of the lion, the king of beasts. The description of the lion also provides a good example of the blend of information provided and the morally didactic element of the text. After a discussion of the lions' habitat and nature, the text explains that cubs are born dead, and after three days their father breathes on them to bring them to life, in an analogy to God's resurrection of Christ.

The sequential description of animals provided a natural opportunity for illustrations of them. This copy is one of the grandest survivals, with eighty paintings of animals on shimmering gold backgrounds. Judging from the expense that would have been incurred in producing such a book, it seems likely that it was intended for an aristocratic, if not royal, layman (or woman) who either could read Latin or had a chaplain to do so for him and his household. It later found a home in the Old Royal library with the purchase by Charles II of the library of the antiquarian John Theyer (d. 1673).

Bestiary with Theological Texts
Central or northern England, *c.* 1200–10
220 x 160 mm
British Library, Royal 12 C. xix, f. 6

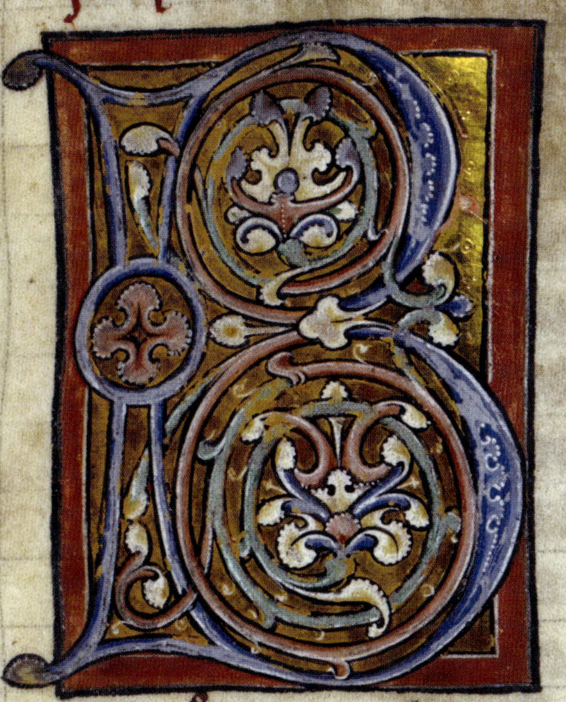

bulum ppie auenit
leonibz. pardis z tigribz.
lupis z uulpibz. cani
bus z simijs. ursibz
z cetis que ul ore ul
unguibz seuiunt. ex
ceptis serpentibz. Bes
tie aute dicte au q
seuiunt. fere appella

te eo qd naturali utuntur libertate. z desiderio
suo ferant. Sunt eni libere eox uoluntates z
huc atq; illuc uagant. Et quo animus duxe
rit: eo ferantur. De naturis Leonum.

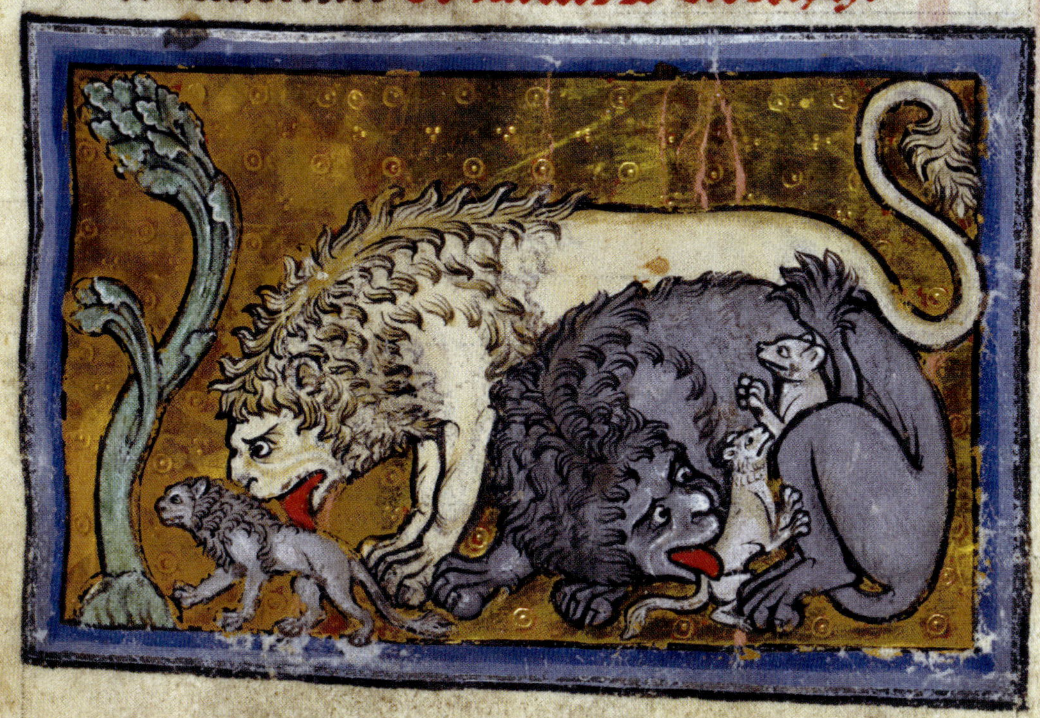

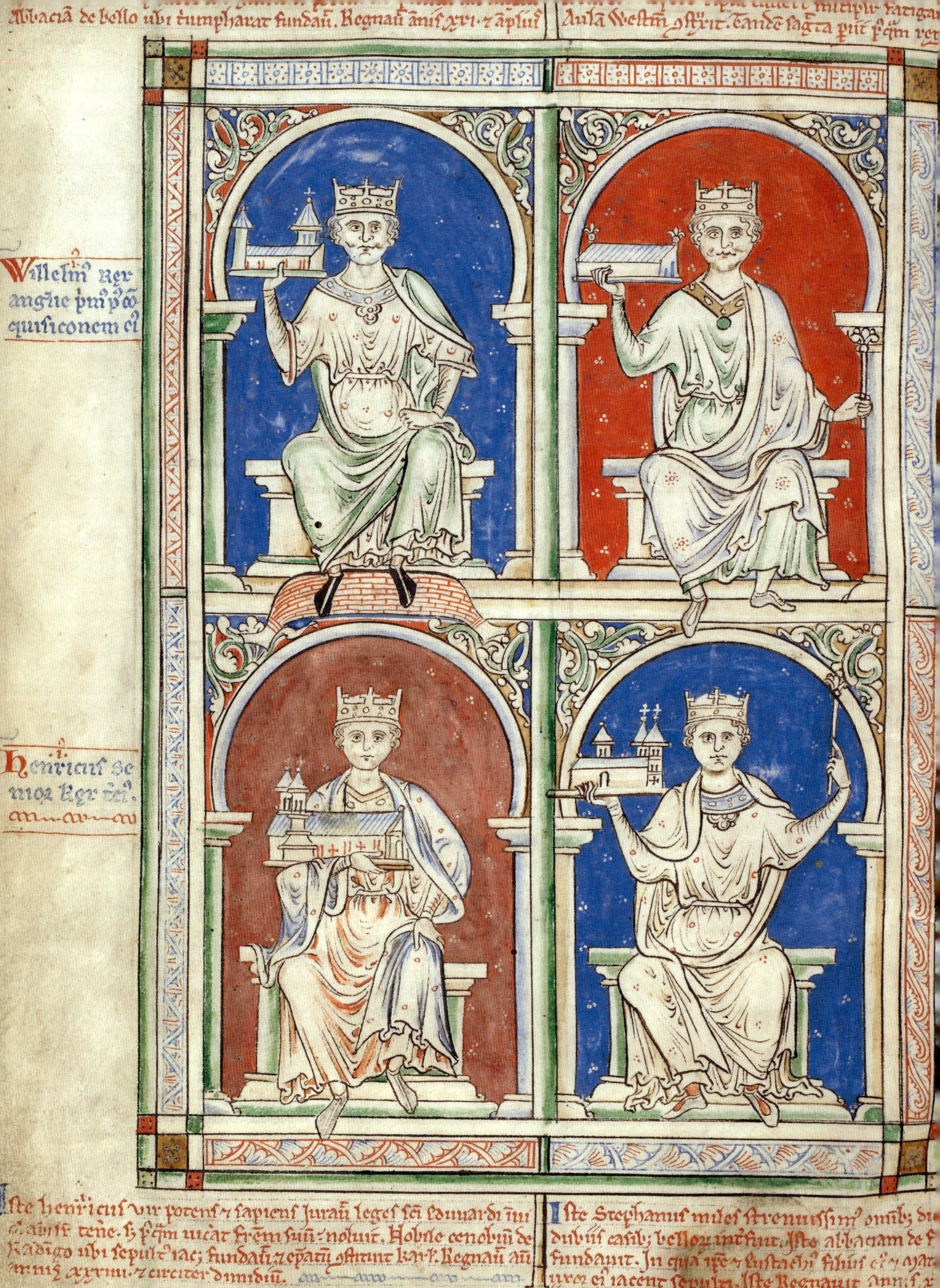

Iste Henricus vir potens et sapiens iurauit leges sancti Eduuardi inuiolabiliter tene. Sed fratrem suum · noluit. Hobile cenobium de Radigo ubi sepulti iacent fundauit et episcopatum constituit karliolensem. Regnauit annis xxxvii et circiter dimidium · | Iste Stephanus miles strenuissimus omnibus dubiis casibus bellorum interfuit. Iste abbaciam de fundauit. In qua ipse et Eustachius filius eius et uxor eius iacent sepulti. Iste Regnauit annis x

7 English kings from William I to Stephen

Matthew Paris (d. *c.* 1259) was one of the foremost English historians of the Middle Ages. He remained a monk of St Albans throughout his adult life, and was often called upon to advise the King, Henry III (r. 1216–72). Matthew's surname may indicate French origins, or more probably that he studied in the schools of Paris when he was young. His principal work was the extensive *Chronica Maiora* (*Greater Chronicle*), an ambitious project covering world history from Creation to the present day. This manuscript is his autograph copy of part of this text, which he also illustrated. The chronicle is bound with another of Paris's histories, the *Historia Anglorum* (*History of the English*), together with various prefatory matter, including the full-page images of kings shown here. The purpose of these kings and their relationship to the text is not entirely clear. However, they do correspond to the historical period covered in the *Historia Anglorum*, which begins with the conquest of England by William the Conqueror and continues to the reign of Henry III.

These eight kings are pictured in a kind of gallery, each labelled, and holding some sort of attribute associated with him. The aspect of kingship Paris has chosen to emphasise is the king's role as patron of monastic foundations and builder. Thus William I holds a model of Battle Abbey, which he founded; William II, the hall at Westminster Palace; Henry I, his foundation of Reading Abbey; Stephen, his abbey of Faversham (these four pictured); Henry II, Waltham Abbey, which he reformed; Richard I, the church of St Thomas of Canterbury that he established at Acre; John, the Cistercian abbey at Beaulieu; and Henry III, his newly built abbey church at Westminster.

Matthew Paris, *Historia Anglorum and Chronica Maiora* (part III)
St Albans, *c.* 1250
360 x 245 mm
British Library, Royal 14 C. vii, f. 8v

8 King David and the arms of England

Like the Westminster Psalter (no. 5), the beginning of Psalms in the Alphonso Psalter is illustrated by an image of a crowned King David playing the harp. Here, however, the image has been placed inside the first letter of the text 'B' (*eatus*) (blessed). This type of 'historiated initial' is characteristic of English illuminated manuscripts of the twelfth and thirteenth centuries. Also characteristic of the later thirteenth century is the solid 'bar' border enclosing the text, and inhabited by interesting scenes and creatures. On this page birds perch around the edges, while in the lower margin David prepares to launch his slingshot against a heavily armed and giant Goliath.

The arms in the centre of the lower margin identify the intended recipient of this copy of the Psalms as Prince Alphonso (b. 1273, d. 1284), the second son and heir apparent of Edward I (r. 1272–1307) and Eleanor of Castile, named after his grandfather Alfonso X of Castile and León. The arms of England, on the left, are coupled with those of Holland and Zeeland, on the right, representing Margaret, daughter of Florent V, Count of Holland and Zeeland, to whom Alphonso was betrothed in 1284. Unfortunately, the young Prince died a few months before the wedding was scheduled to take place; the decoration of this opulent Psalter was left unfinished as a result. It was completed a decade later in 1297, when Alphonso's sister Elizabeth married John I of Holland and Zeeland, the brother of Alphonso's intended bride, making the pairing of arms and the Psalter again appropriate for a royal wedding.

The Alphonso Psalter
London, *c.* 1284 (ff. 11–25v), with later additions
245 x 165 mm
British Library, Additional 24686, f. 11

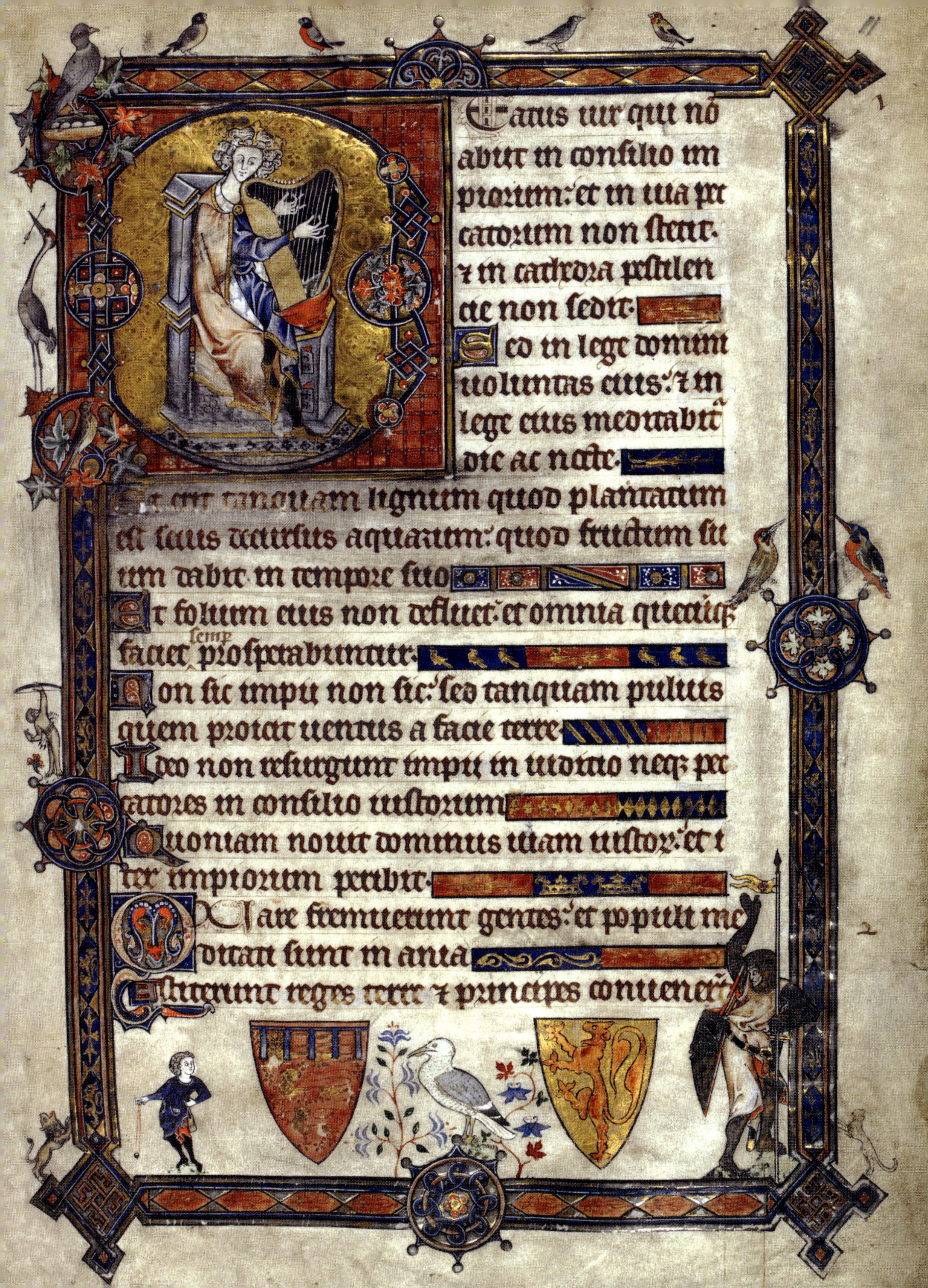

Eatus uir qui non
abiit in consilio im
piorum: et in uia pec
catorum non stetit:
z in cathedra pestilen
cie non sedit.
Sed in lege domini
uoluntas eius: z in
lege eius meditabit
die ac nocte.
Et erit tanquam lignum quod plantatum
est secus decursus aquarum: quod fructum su
um dabit in tempore suo.
Et folium eius non defluet: et omnia quecumq;
faciet prosperabuntur.
Non sic impii non sic: sed tanquam puluis
quem proicit uentus a facie terre.
Ideo non resurgunt impii in iudicio neq; pec
catores in consilio iustorum.
Quoniam nouit dominus uiam iustorum: et i
ter impiorum peribit.
Quare fremuerunt gentes: et populi me
ditati sunt inania.
Astiterunt reges terre z principes conuenert̃

9 Instructions for knights

Texts on warfare that might provide insights for knights were amongst the most popular of secular texts in the medieval period. This French translation of the treatise on Roman warfare, *De re militari*, written by Flavius Vegetius Renatus (fl. *c.* 383–450) is one of six copies of versions of Vegetius that were recorded in the Old Royal library at Westminster Palace in 1542. The French translation and adaptation, known as the *Les establissemens de chevalerie* (*Institutions of Knighthood*), was completed in 1284; another adaptation of *De re militari* in Anglo-Norman French was written for Prince Edward, later Edward I (1272–1307) around this same time.

This manuscript has only one illustration, at the beginning of the first book, but it is an elegant and sophisticated complement to the text. The image conflates two episodes. On the left, Vegetius presents his new composition to a Roman emperor, in a practice described in the preceding preface. To the right, two of the military exercises outlined in the treatise are pictured, arrayed as knights in contemporary dress. In the centre, one practises at the 'pile' (or 'pale'), a wooden pole used for training with sword and shield, adopted as part of medieval jousts. To the right, another knight attempts to mount his horse in full armour. Interestingly, this unusual combination of scenes appears in three other copies of *Les establissemens de chevalerie*. The illustration seems to have been developed in Paris especially to accompany Jean de Meun's new translation.

Jean de Meun, *Les establissemens de chevalerie*
(French translation of Vegetius, *De re militari*)
Paris, *c.* 1300
260 x 165 mm
British Library, Royal 20 B. xi, f. 3 (detail)

ta bonne volente pour le sauuement du gnuu enst les tai
drent z garderent iadis al qui firent lempir de rome.
Et que tu puisses trouuer en cest petit liuret. tout quã
que tu tdoit quelen die quatre des choses tres grans. et
qui touz iours out mestier li deffendre lonneur de leu
pir de rome.

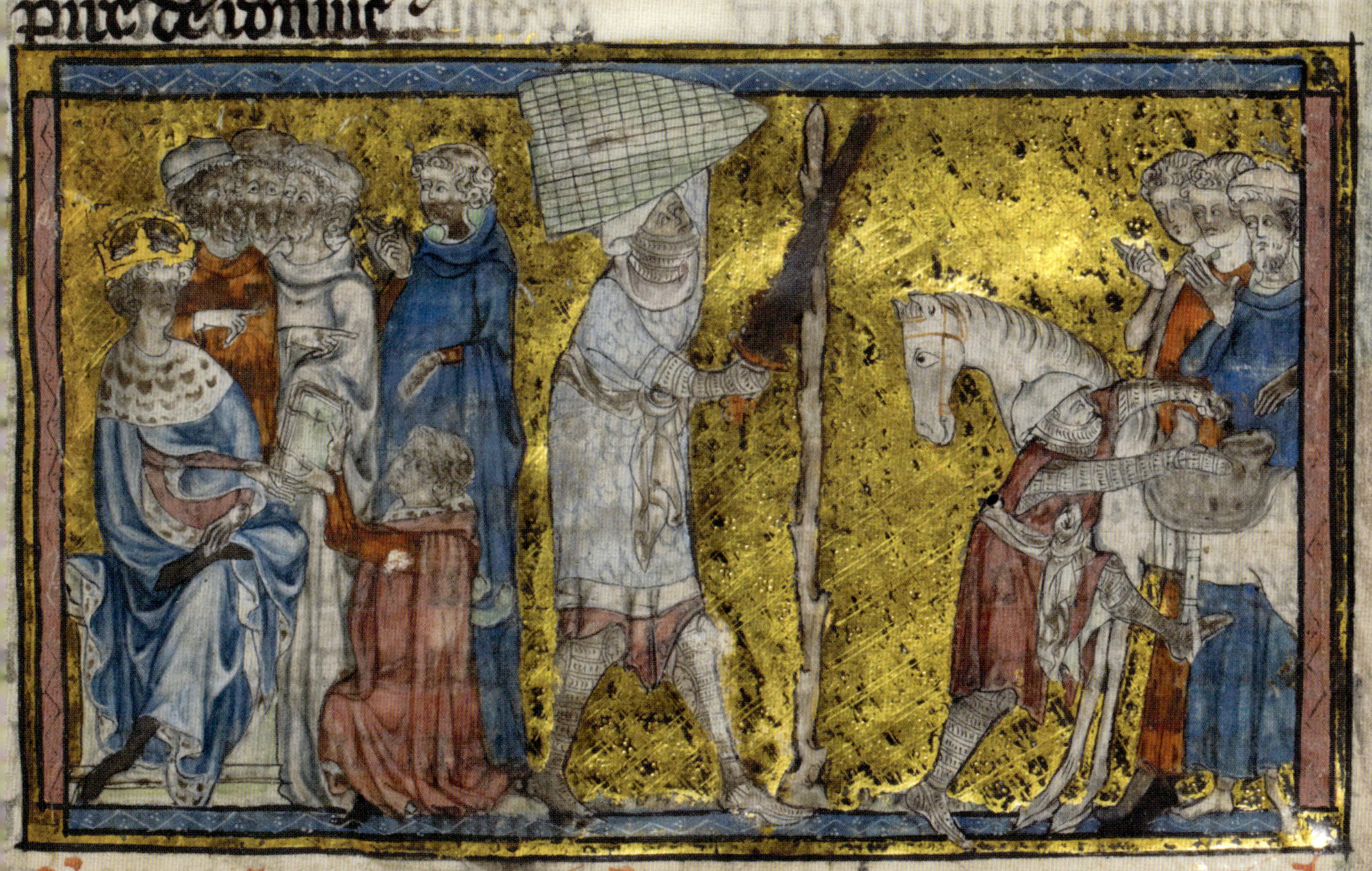

10 Genealogy of William the Conqueror

Unlike most other texts, chronicles of English history were presented both in codex or book form (see nos. 7 and 11) and in a roll format on sheets of parchment glued together end to end. This format was ideal for the presentation of history as genealogy or a royal family tree, with detailed long diagrams of royal descent featuring kings and members of their families in roundels. The present copy is nearly five metres long. These rolls were particularly popular in England in the late thirteenth and fourteenth centuries, with around forty surviving from between the time of Edward I's accession in 1272 to the end of Henry V's reign in 1422. In these copies the chronicle is presented as short captions to the images and as a running commentary, typically in Anglo-Norman French, the language of the English aristocracy throughout the Middle Ages.

The first king to feature in this roll is Egbert (d. 839), the King of Wessex who united the Anglo-Saxon kingdoms. The line (pictured) starts again with Rollo, 1st Duke of Normandy (d. *c.* 932), descending to William 1 (r. 1066–87) or 'William the Bastard' as he was then known and labelled thus in the roll (the lowest roundel pictured). With William the roll is further decorated with two large trees and lush vegetation, inhabited by various animals including two rabbits, perhaps an allusion to the fecundity of the Norman line. The royal line continues in the original hand to Edward I, with Edward II and Edward III added by a later scribe. The number, language and complexity of production of these rolls suggest that they were popular with aristocratic and royal patrons as a graphic visual aid to the learning of history and the role and identity of kings.

Genealogical Chronicle of English Kings
England (East Anglia?), *c.* 1300–07
4750 x 275 mm
British Library, Royal 14 B. vi (detail)

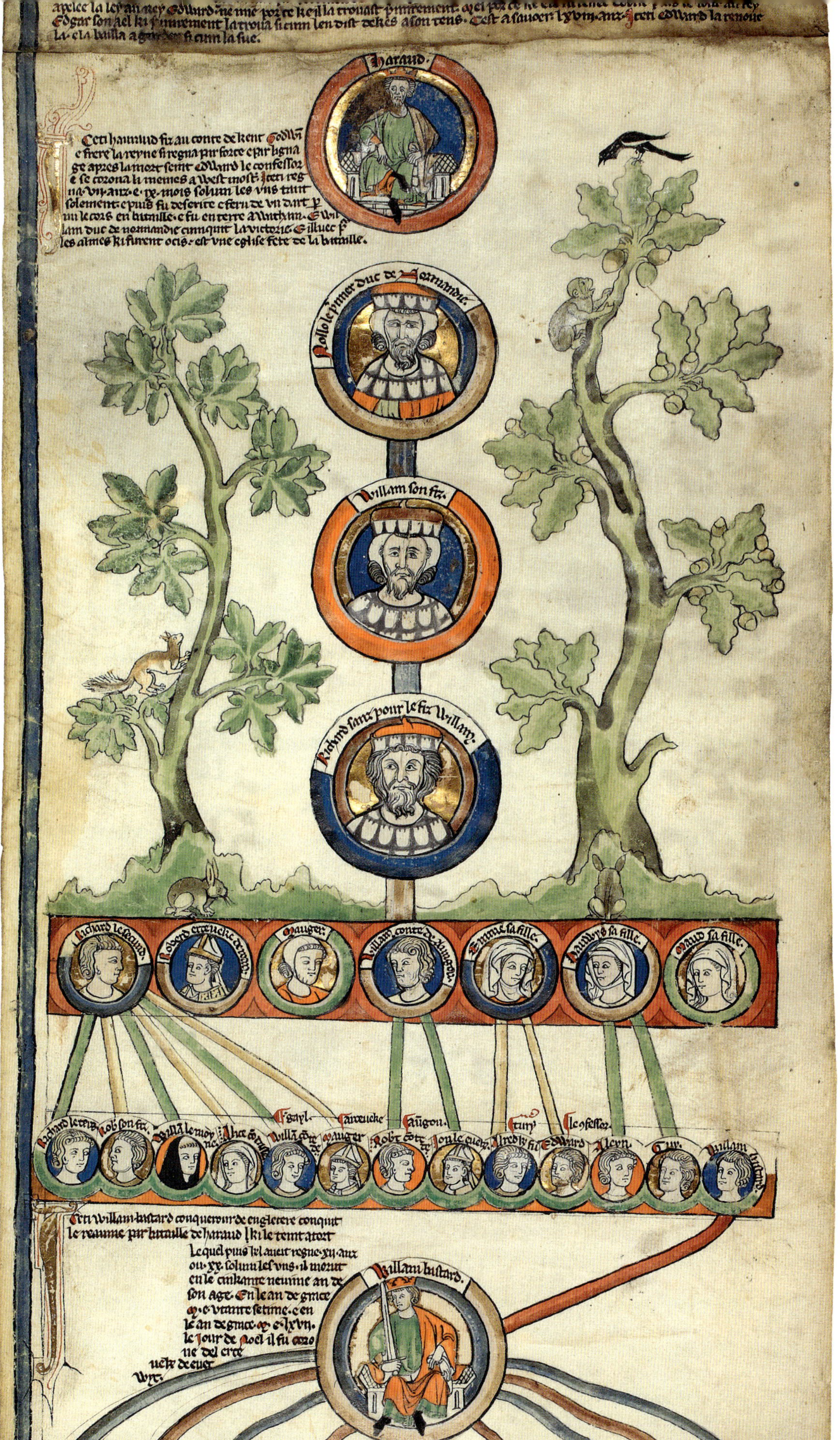

apelee la lei an rey Edward me mie poi re ke il la trouast primerement. ... poi ... kil la rennie si enn len dist. dekes a son tens. Cest a sauoer ... rey Edward la renoue la e la bailla a garder si enn la sue.

Haraud.

Cesti Haruund fiz au conte de Kent Godwi
e frere la reyne si regna par force e par signa
ge apres la mort seint Edward le confessor
e se corona li memes a West mostr. Icesti reg
na vii anz e x mois solum les uns tant
solement. e puis fu desconfite e feru de un dart p
mi le cors en bataille. e fu enterre a Waltham. Guil
lam duc de Normandie enquint la victorie. E illuec s
les almes ki furent ocis. est une eglise fete de la bataille.

Rollo le primer duc de Normundie.

Willam son fiz.

Richard sanz pour le fiz Willam.

Richard le secund. Robert erceueske de Roan. Mauger. Willam conte de Hungol. Emme sa fille. Maud sa fille. Maud sa fille.

Richard le terz. Rob son fiz. Willa le moygne. Iohan sa fille. Esayl. Willa conte de Mauger. Warenche. Robt cotte. Augon. Ion le eues. Aldredy fiz. Turi. Edward. le Confessor. Aleyn. Tur. Willam bastard.

Cesti William bastard conquerour de Engletere conquit
le reaume par bataille de Haraud ki le tenit a tort
Le quel puis kil aueit regne xxi anz
ou xx. solum les uns. il morut
en le cinkante neuime an de
son age. En le an de grace
M. C. vi vante setime. e en
le an de grace M. C. lxvii.
le jour de Noel il fu coro
ne del cre
ue ke de euer
wyk.

Willam bastard.

11 King Arthur

Peter of Langtoft (d. *c.* 1305), an Augustinian canon at Bridlington in Yorkshire, composed a chronicle of the history of Britain in Anglo-Norman French. The text's survival in twenty-one copies indicates that it must have been one of the most popular French chronicles after the *Brut d'Engleterre*, and Wace's *Brut* chronicles. The present copy is unusual in that it includes a series of twenty full-page illustrations of English kings before the beginning of the text.

The kings start with Brutus, the legendary exile from Troy and first king of Britain, and include Arthur, shown here. Rather surprisingly, given his later popularity and prominence in Arthurian romances, images of Arthur are rather rare in medieval manuscripts made in England. Here he wears his sword Excalibur and holds a shield decorated with an image of the Virgin Mary. This shield is mentioned in earlier chronicles, such as Geoffrey of Monmouth's *History of the Kings of Britain*, which Langtoft consulted in composing his own chronicle. Langtoft casts Arthur as a model of a Christian king, and reports that his crown and sword were used by later English kings.

With its gallery of kings (compare no. 7), it would have been appropriate for this illustrated version of the chronicle to be part of the Old Royal library. However, like the Matthew Paris manuscript, this one may not have been intended for a royal owner. It was present in the royal library at Westminster (Whitehall) Palace by 1542, and may have been sequestered by Henry VIII together with many other historical and biblical manuscripts.

Peter of Langtoft's *Chronicle, the Lament of Edward II*, fragments
of Romances, and a letter attributed to Joanna, Queen of Sicily
Northern England, *c.* 1307–27
230 x 150 mm
British Library, Royal 20 A. ii, f. 4

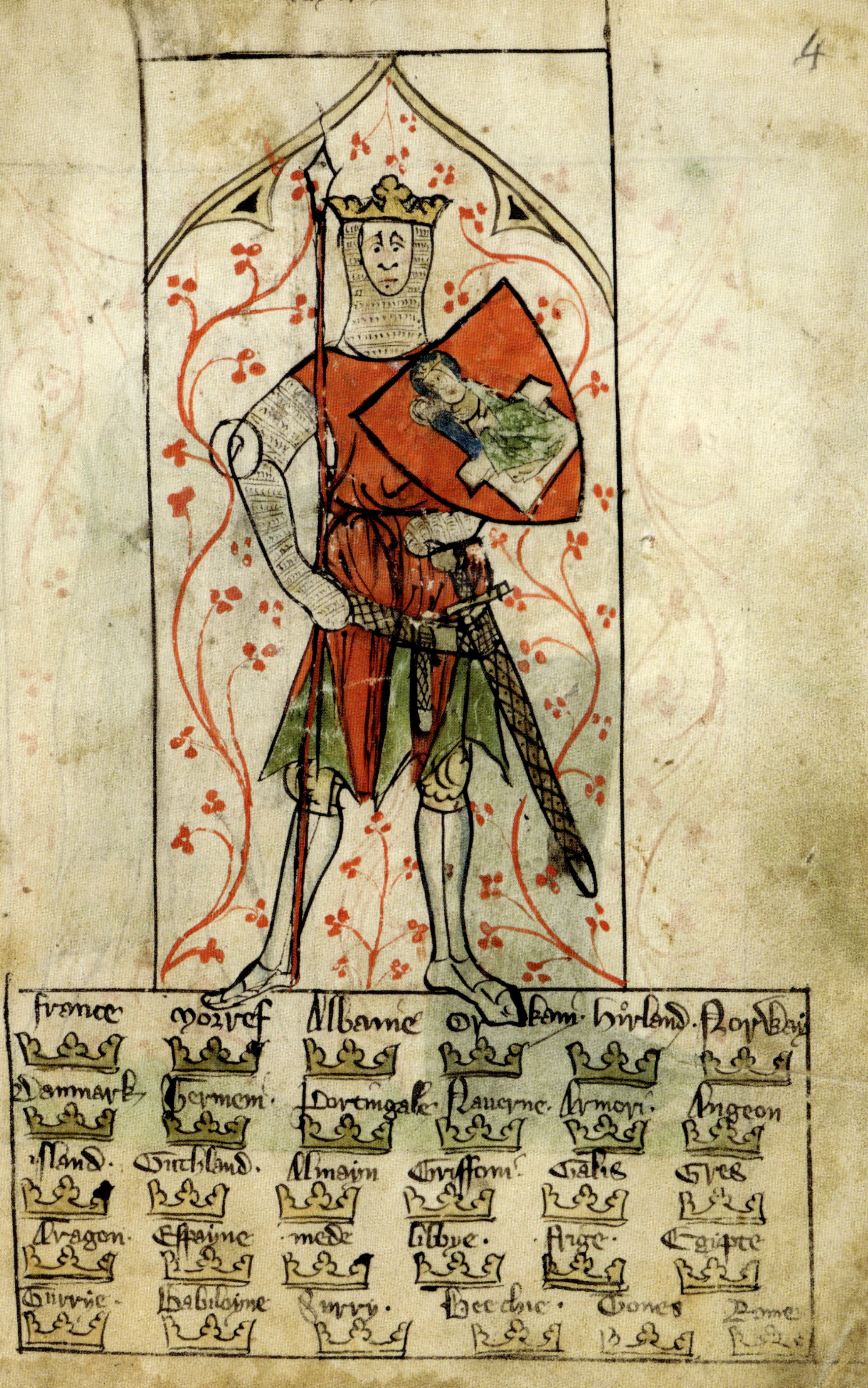

france   yorvef   Albanie   or Scom hirland   Roybay
Denmark   Germen   Portingale   Nauerne   Armori   Angeon
ylland   Sutchland   Almain   Gryffom   Galis   Gres
Aragon   Espaine   mede   libye   Arge   Egipte
Surrye   babiloine   Surri   Beechic   Tones   Rome

12 Gideon refusing the crown

As is evident from many of the manuscripts featured in this book, not all of the books in the Old Royal library were commissioned by kings or queens for their own use. Perhaps the most famous and certainly the most lavishly illustrated example of a late arrival to the Library is the Queen Mary Psalter, which has been called the 'most beautiful manuscript in the whole collection'. Its title derives from the circumstances of its presentation to Queen Mary Tudor in 1553 by Baldwin Smith, a quick-thinking customs official who rescued it from exportation after the arrest of its owner.

The manuscript has over one thousand illustrations – at least one on every page, executed in a variety of media. These comprise various series of scenes running along the lower margin, as well as illustrated initials and Psalms, in addition to full-page images of the Life of Christ, and even more rarely, of Old Testament scenes at the beginning of the book, delicately executed in ink with light colour washes. Here, for example, Gideon (called Jerubbaal in the captions, meaning 'contender with Baal', referring to his destruction of the altar of Baal), commands his son Jether to execute the Midianite kings Zebah and Zalumna. These kings are imposing crowned figures standing to the left in the upper part of the image. However, the boy was frightened and 'would not draw his sword', so Gideon instead executed the kings himself (Judges 8:19). Below, the Israelites are shown attempting to anoint Gideon as a king and offering him a sceptre and crown.

Overleaf, part of the Life of Christ, the Warning of the Magi not to return to Herod (Matthew 2:12) and the Slaughter of the Innocents (Matthew 2:16) is illustrated above one of the major divisions of the Psalms. Psalm 38 begins with the verse 'I said: I will take heed to my ways: that I sin not with my tongue.' The artist has interpreted this verse literally with a praying king pointing to his mouth (or perhaps tongue).

The Queen Mary Psalter
London (?), c. 1310–20
275 x 175 mm
British Library, Royal 2 B. vii, f. 37; overleaf, ff. 131v–132

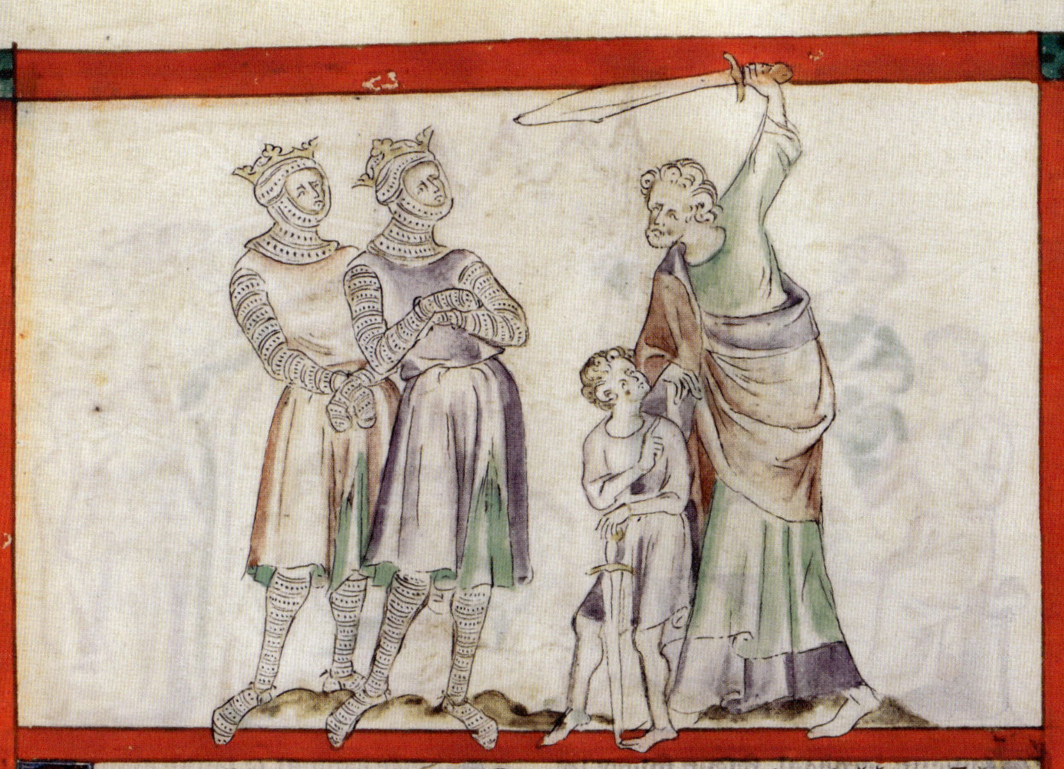

Coment Jeroboal comandoit son fiz occire ces deus Reys. E il li dit q'il ne
oillt pas le per. E li memes les allat occire.

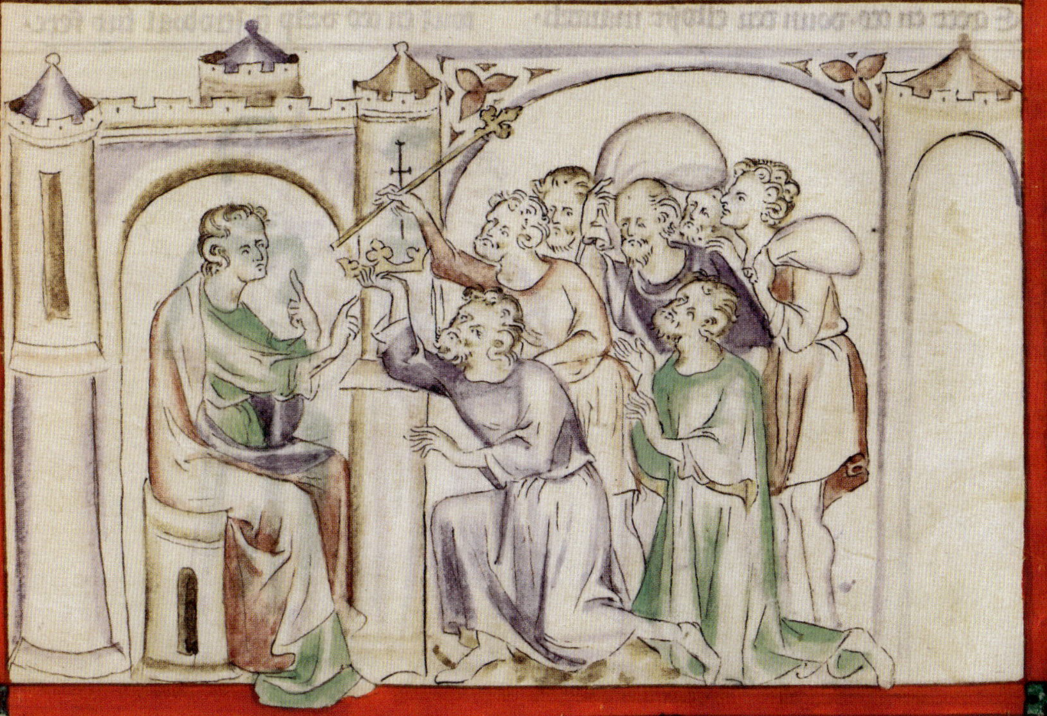

Coment le gentz de Israel venoient a Jerobo
al e li voleient fere Rey e seignour. E li offi-
rent coroune de Reyaute. E verge de seignrie.

Coment Jeroboal les envoi
ast quere les ancles qe estoient
de deuz les orayles occis. ·~·~·

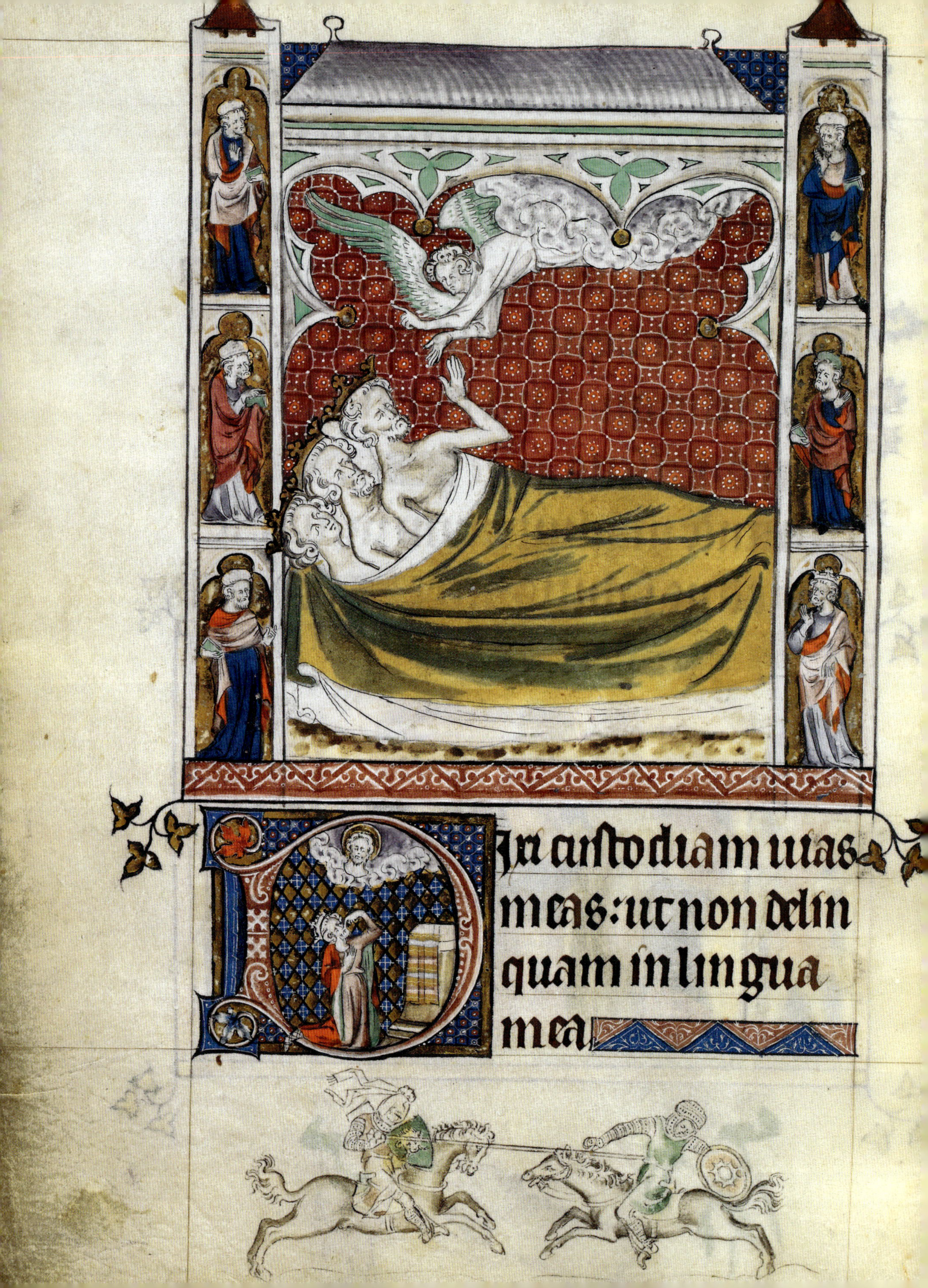

in custodiam uias
meas: ut non delin
quam in lingua
mea

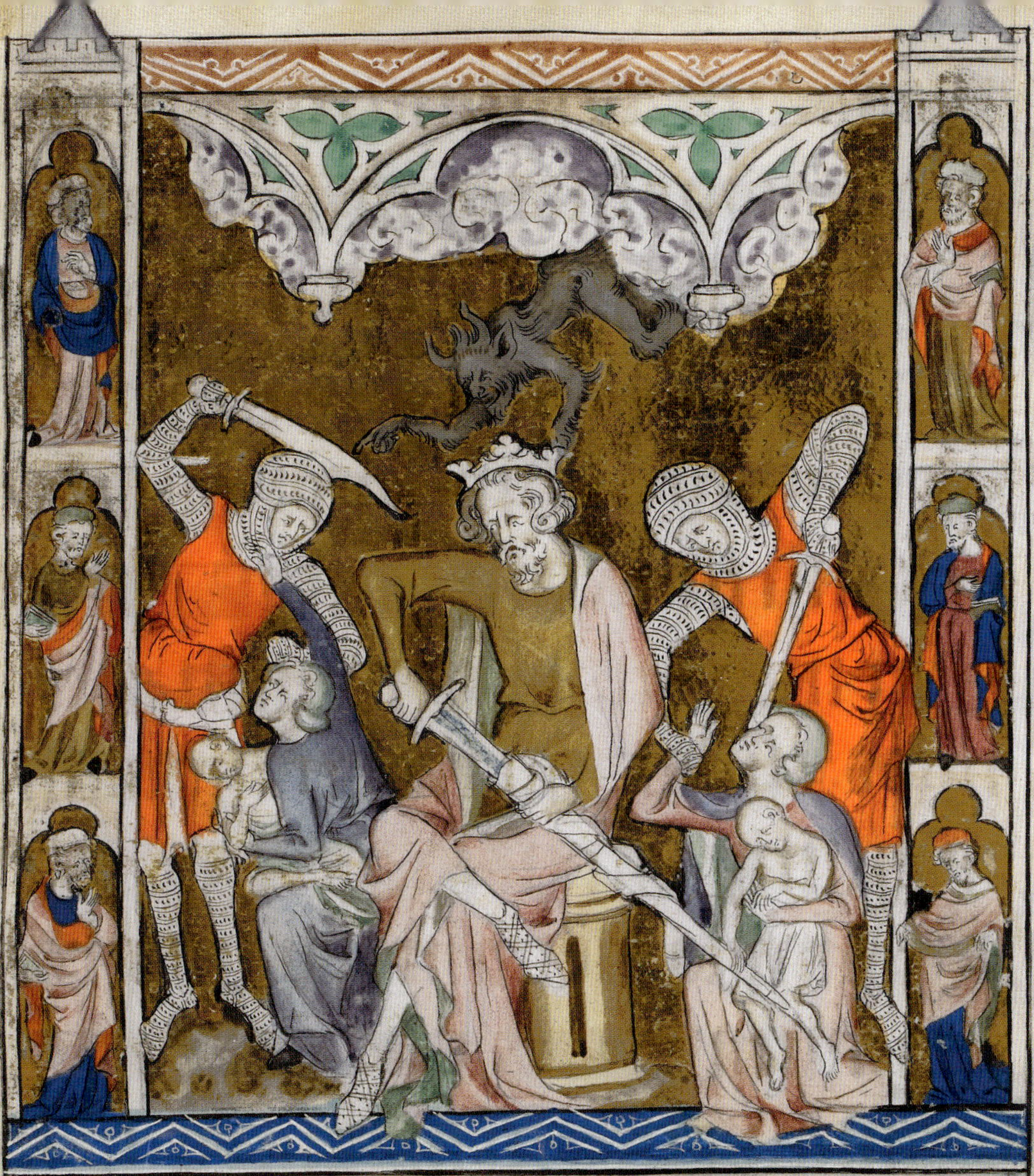

Posui ori meo custodiam: cum con
sisteret peccator aduersum me.
Obmutui et humiliatus sum. et si
lui a bonis: et dolor meus renouatus est.

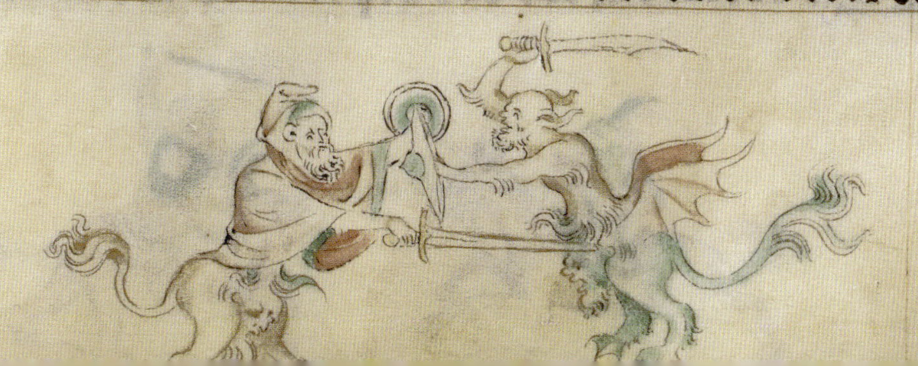

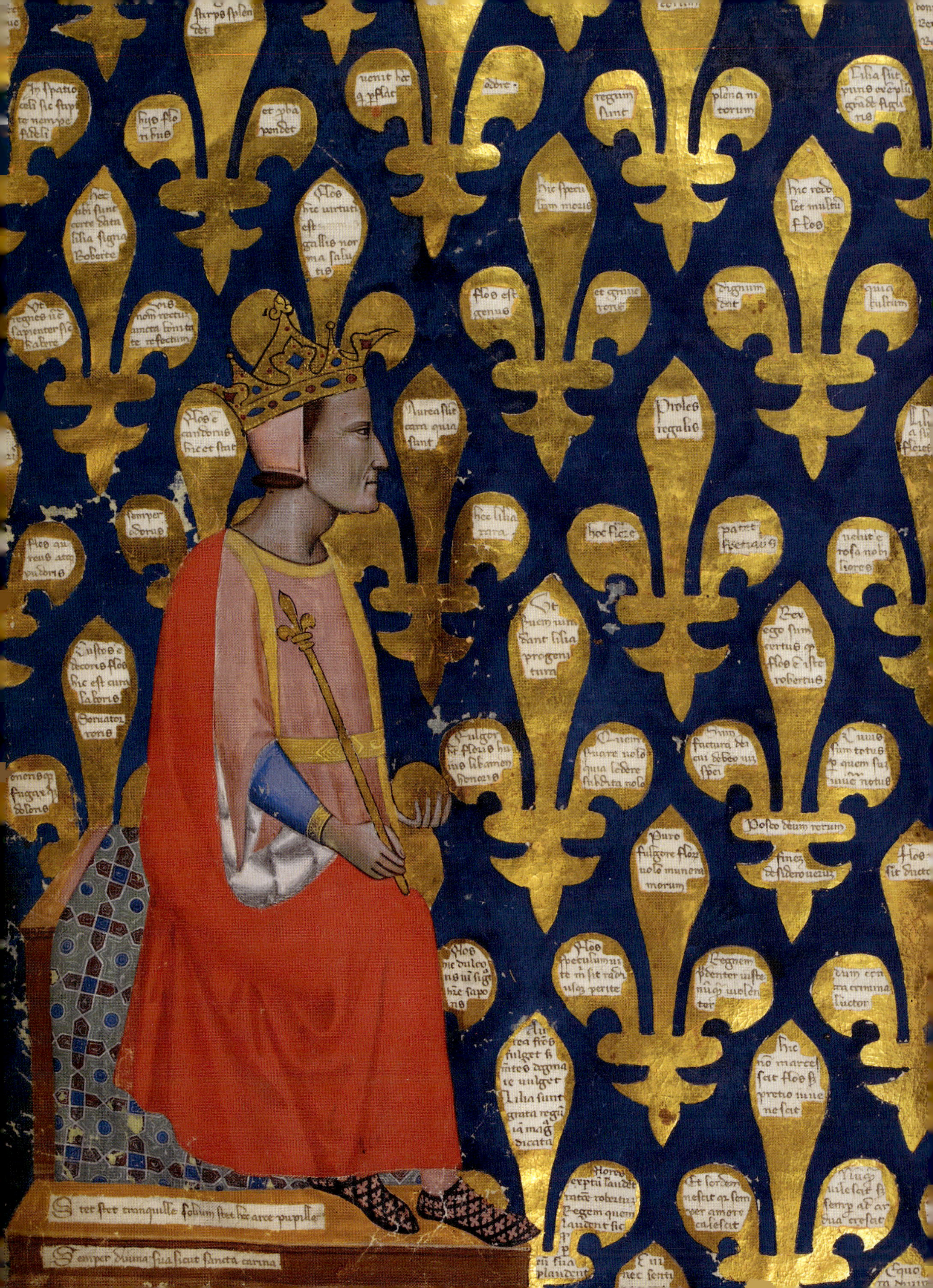
Stet stet tranquille folium stet hec arce pupille
Semper diuina fua ficut fancta carina

13 Robert of Anjou, King of Naples, enthroned

This spectacular image of kingship occurs in a work of Latin verse that survives in only three copies. The present copy is huge in scale, at nearly half a metre in height (around 1 ½ ft), and is also the grandest of the three surviving manuscripts in the scope of its illustration and richness of decorative detail. It may have been the presentation copy for Robert of Anjou, King of Naples (r. 1309–43), the addressee of the poems from the city of Prato. The fleurs-de-lis in the background refer to the Anjou family's position as a cadet branch of the Capetian ruling family of France. The city, personified in the poem, beseeches Robert for protection, to unite Italy, and to restore the papacy to Rome from Avignon, where it had moved in 1309.

The originality and scale of the work and its illustrations must have been well-received by Robert, a renowned bibliophile (though it did not move him to act on the citizens' requests). The manuscript's path to the English Old Royal library is less clear. Several Angevin manuscripts entered the libraries of Charles V (r. 1364–80), and his brother John, Duke of Berry (b. 1340, d. 1416). The entire French royal library at the Louvre was acquired by the English general John, Duke of Bedford (b. 1389, d. 1435), following the death of Charles VI. Bedford served as Regent of France on behalf of the infant English King Henry VI (r. 1422–61), so perhaps this magnificent royal book became the property of the English kings through Bedford's offices.

Carmina regia: Address of the City of Prato to Robert of Anjou
Tuscany, *c.* 1335
480 x 340 mm
British Library, Royal 6 E. ix, f. 10v

14 God and the four Evangelists

On 19 September 1356 Edward, the Black Prince (d. 1376), the eldest son of
Edward II (r. 1327–77), chose a favourable battlefield position to confront the
French king, John II the Good (r. 1350–64) and a formidable French army outside
of Poitiers. Harried by English archers, by the end of the day the Dauphin, heir to
the French throne, had fled, and John the Good had surrendered. Some months
later the Black Prince escorted his prisoner to London, together with other captives
and the spoils of the battle, which included this elegant copy of the *Bible historiale.*
An inscription records that 'this book was taken with the King of France at the
Battle of Poitiers, and the good Count of Salisbury, William Montagu, bought it
for 100 marks and gave it to his wife Elisabeth'.

The handsome book is a copy of the most common version of the Bible in French,
known as the *Bible historiale* or history Bible, which combines sections of the Latin
version of the Bible, the Vulgate, with commentary or gloss interpreting the
biblical text together with other historical events. These vernacular historicised
Bibles were often abundantly illustrated. Here the Bible opens with an image of
God surrounded by the symbols of the Four Evangelists, painted by the same artist
as the following manuscript (no. 15). Below this main scene Samson carries the
gates of Gaza (Judges 16:3), and to the right, Solomon determines the true son
from amongst three claimants, as the man who refused to shoot an arrow at his
father's corpse.

Bible historiale
Paris, *c.* 1350 (before 1356)
420 x 285 mm
British Library, Royal 19 D. ii, f. 1

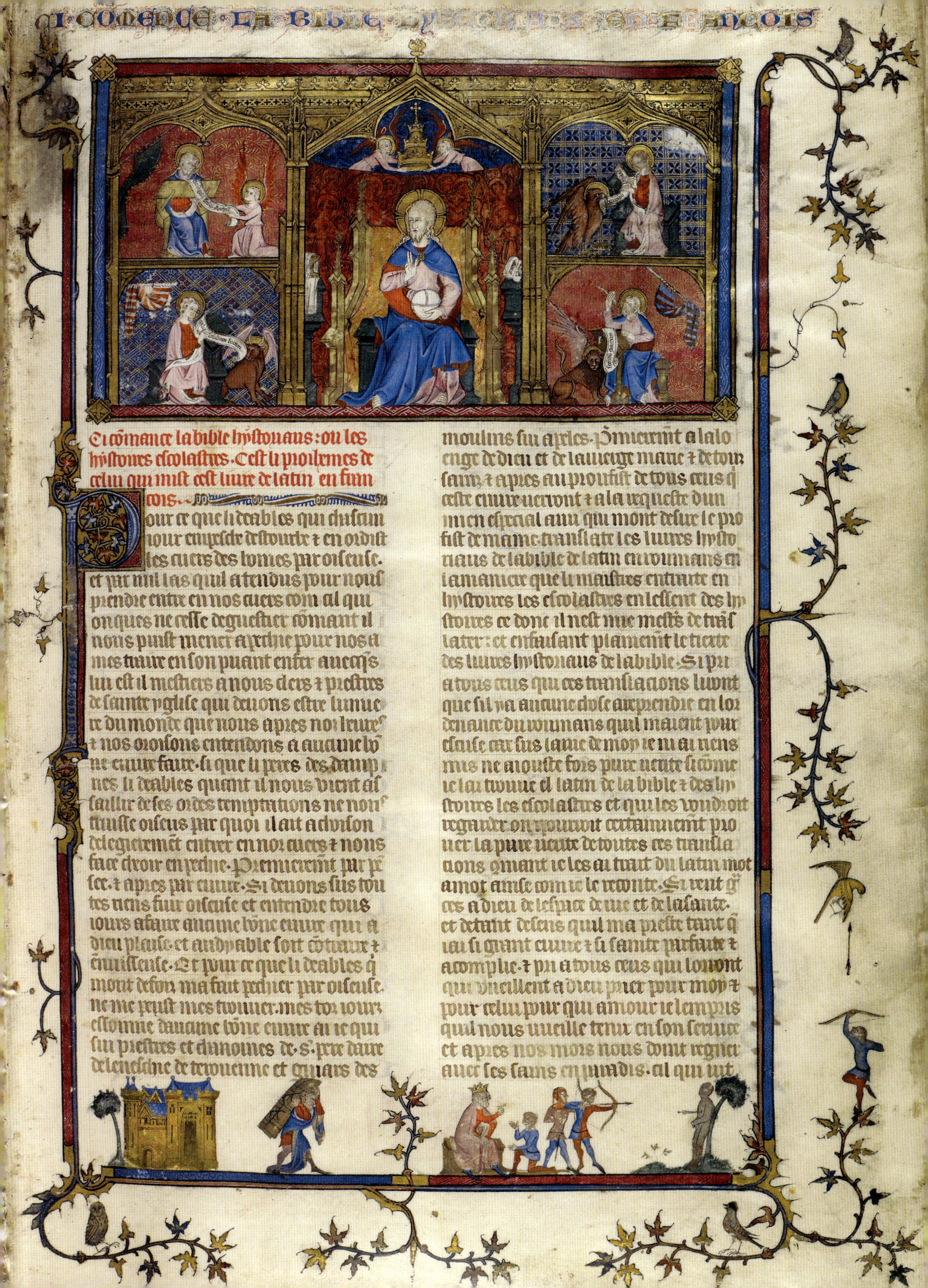

euntes. ita et interius animo sapientie uir-
tutumq; geminis decorari contendas. qua-
tinus post occasum huius seculi cum pruden-
tibz uirginibz sponso perhenni dño nro ihe-
su xpo digne et laudabiliter occurrens regi-
am celestis aule merearis ingredi ianuam
Auxiliante dño nro. Post impositam coronam
Omnium dñe fons dicat archiepiscopus
bonoꝛ et cunctoꝛ datoꝛ prouectuum
tribue famule tue. ꝗ. adeptam bene regere
dignitatem. et a te sibi prestitam in ea
bonis operibz corrobora gliam. per d.

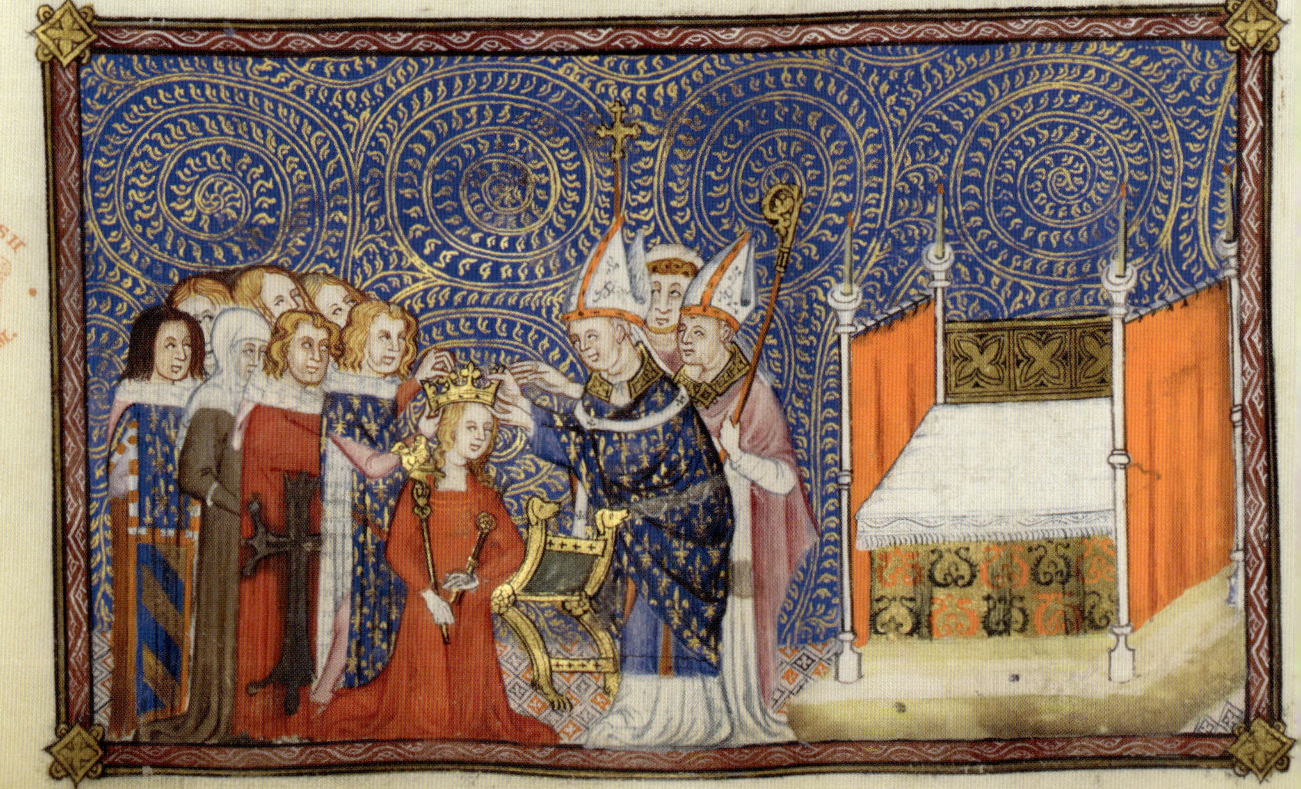

15 The coronation of Queen Jeanne de Bourbon

The Coronation Book of Charles V (r. 1364–80) is an extraordinary illustrated record of the coronation ceremony of the King and of his wife, Jeanne de Bourbon. It is Charles's personal copy, which he signed and dated recording that he had ordered the book to be 'arranged, written, corrected and illustrated' a year after his ceremony took place. The account was an idealised version, reflecting how the ceremonies should have been performed, and departing in part from accounts of what actually occurred. It probably informed later coronation ceremonies: for example, Charles's son Charles VI (r. 1380–1422) took it with him to his own coronation at Reims cathedral.

The manuscript is extensively illustrated. On virtually every page a detailed scene accompanies the description of the ceremony. These paintings were completed by one of Charles's favourite artists, known as the Master of the Coronation Book, from this book. The paintings of Charles are portraits, while the various courtiers and officials who participated in the ceremony can be identified only by their heraldic devices. Here the Queen is shown being crowned by the Archbishop of Reims, with the barons supporting or 'sustaining' this action by reaching out to touch the crown. The Queen's ceremony differed from the King's in that she received a short rod and the so-called sceptre of Dagobert (pictured) instead of the King's *main de justice* and the sceptre of Charlemagne, reflecting that under then current interpretations of Salic law (written around the time of Clovis [r. 476–96] for the Salian Franks), as a woman she would be unable to rule in her own right.

Coronation Book of Charles V (*Livre du sacre des rois de France*)
Paris, 1365
280 x 190 mm
British Library, Cotton Tiberius B. viii, f. 69v

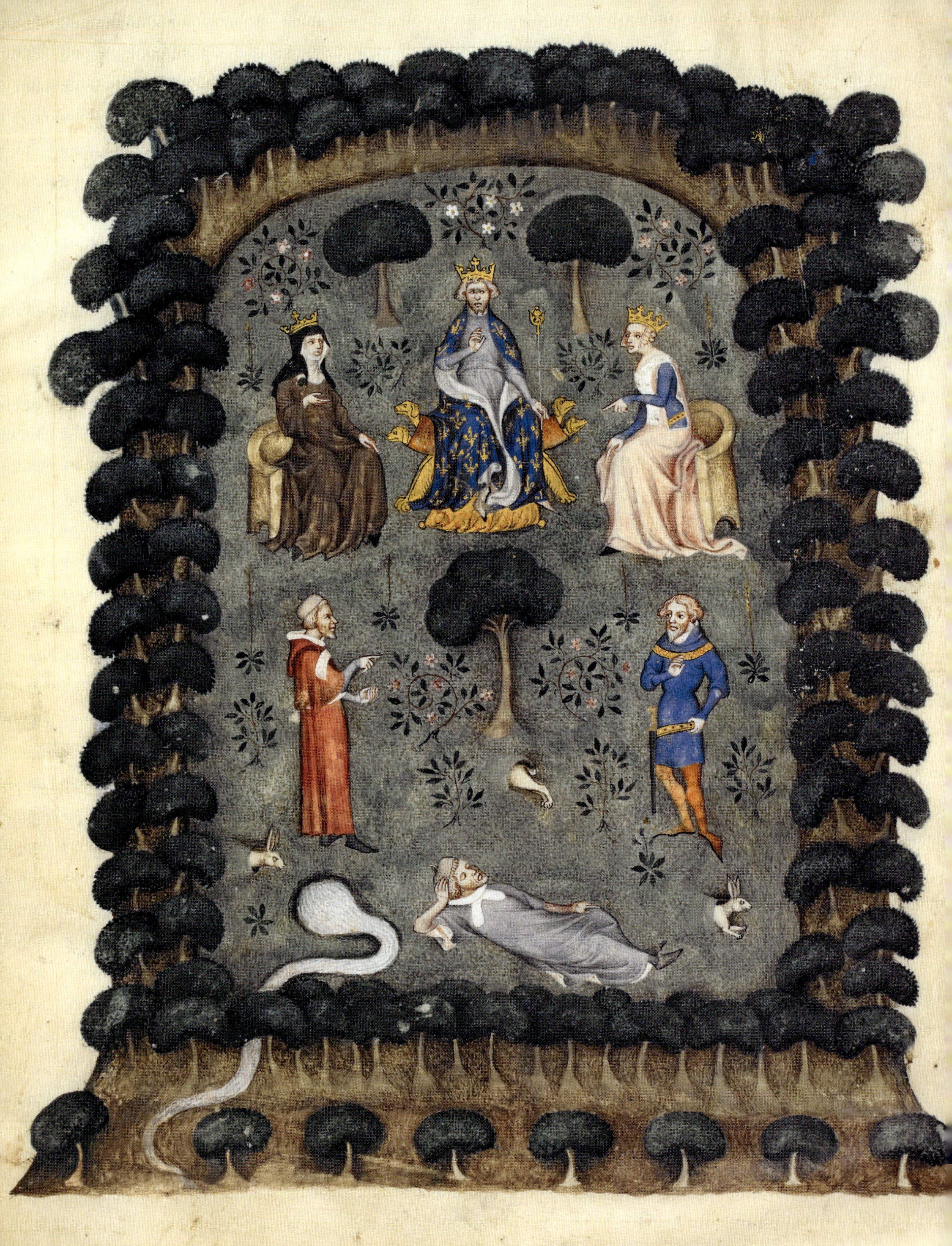

16 Charles V adjudicating

In 1374 Charles V of France (r. 1364–80) commissioned this work on the relationship between secular and ecclesiastical power. After its composition, the King then requested that the Latin text be translated into French, and it became known as *Le Songe du Vergier* (The Dream of the Orchard). It is one of over thirty translations of edifying texts with historical and political subjects that were sponsored by Charles. This impressive copy was the one presented to the King, who is pictured receiving the book in the image opposite the one shown here. Like the previous manuscript that records his coronation ceremony (no. 15), Charles signed this volume.

The full-page illustration at the beginning of the text serves as an introduction to and summary of it. The dialogue or debate is structured in the form of a dream that the author had after having falling asleep in an orchard. Charles V is seen judging the debate between personifications of spiritual and secular power, each crowned. The spiritual power, on the left, is dressed in the brown habit of a Franciscan. Below them, their respective advocates, a cleric and a knight, stand before Charles. A now erased inscription shows that the French royal book was once owned by another great bibliophile, Humfrey, Duke of Gloucester (b. 1390, d. 1447), the youngest of the four sons of Henry IV (r. 1399–1413) who presumably obtained it from his brother John, Duke of Bedford (b. 1389, d. 1435) (see nos. 13 and 21).

Le Songe du Vergier
Paris, 1378
325 x 245 mm
British Library, Royal 19 C. iv, f. 1v

17 Louis of Guyenne receiving instruction from St Louis

During the Middle Ages a genre of text developed to instruct princes on how to be effective rulers. These writings are known collectively as 'mirrors for princes' because they provide exemplars of behaviour, both positive and negative, for the prince to use as a mirror to illuminate his own conduct (compare no. 21).

The *Gesta Sancti Ludovici et Regis Philippi* (the *Deeds of St Louis and King Philip*) is a text in this tradition. This is made explicit in the prologue to the work, in which the monk and archivist at St-Denis now in Paris explains that it is to be an 'exemplum virtutis quasi speculum' (an example of virtue, as if a mirror). The author originally dedicated his work to King Philip IV of France (r. 1285–1314), intending him to follow the example of his predecessors St Louis (r. 1226–70) and Louis's son, Philip III (r. 1270–85), featured in the text.

In the present copy, the dedication is replaced by an image of Louis, Duke of Guyenne, Dauphin of France (b. 1397, d. 1415), son of Charles VI (r. 1380–1422), seated on the right and receiving instruction directly from St Louis. The Dauphin's identity is confirmed by the presence of the arms of his mother, Isabel of Bavaria, on the far wall, and his own arms of a dolphin quartered with France ancient behind him and at his feet. This copy is contemporary with the English text Hoccleve composed for Prince Henry, the future Henry V (no. 21). Both Prince Henry and Louis of Guyenne played important roles in government around the same time, during the illnesses of their fathers. Perhaps both also looked to their 'mirrors' for guidance in how to serve as Christian princes and rulers (however, the Dauphin died in 1415 and never became king). His younger sister Catherine married Henry (by then Henry V) in 1420; the Dauphin's personalised copy of the *Gesta* may have come to England and into the Old Royal library with this dynastic marriage.

Guillaume de Nangis, *Gesta Sancti Ludovici et Regis Philippi*
Paris, *c*. 1401–15
270 x 185 mm
British Library, Royal 13 B. iii, f. 2

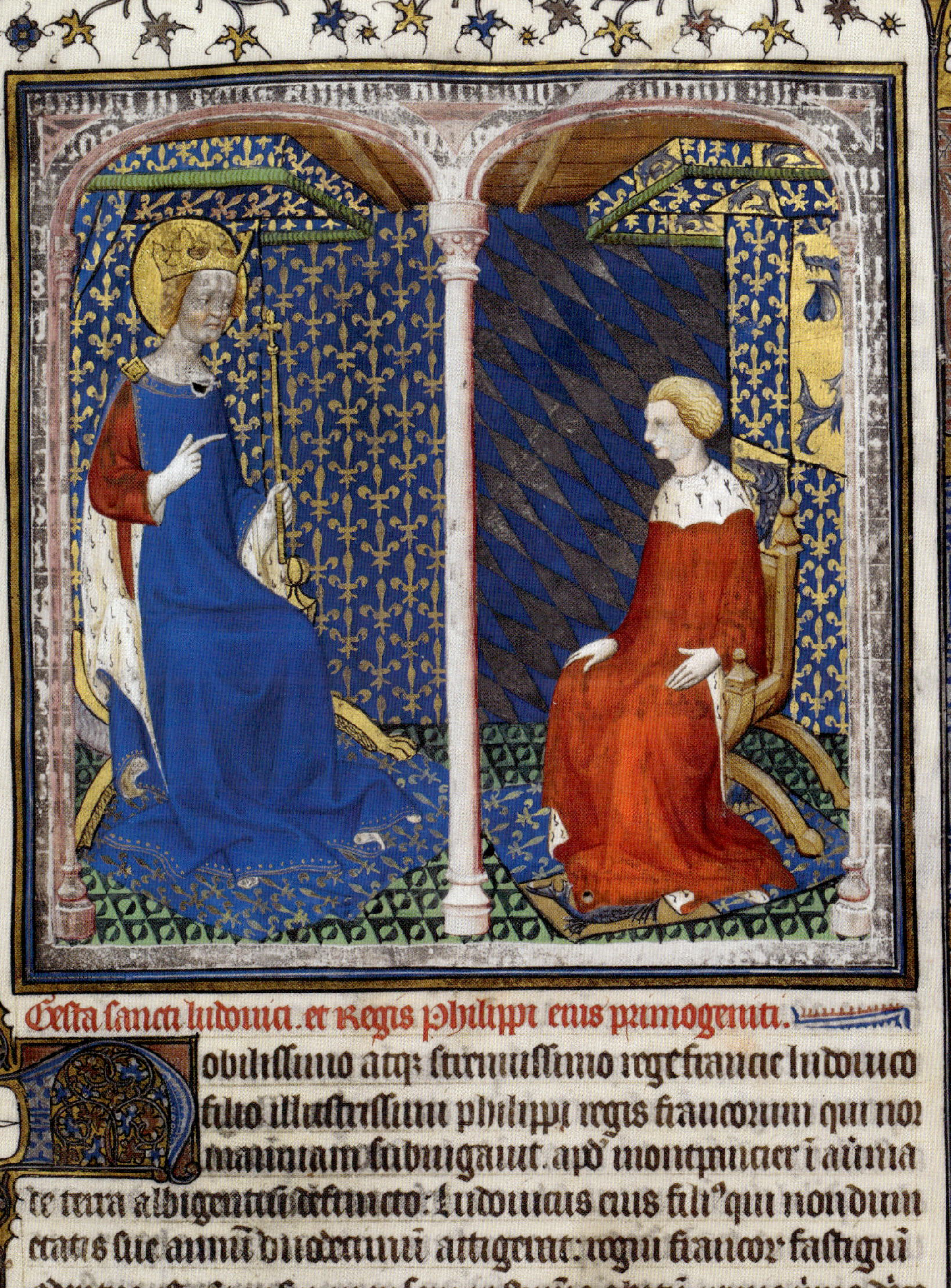

Nobilissimo atq; strenuissimo rege francie ludouico filio illustrissimi philippi regis francorum qui nor maniam subiugauit. apd montpancer i armia te terra albigentis defuncto: ludouicus eius fili' qui nondum etatis sue annum duodecimum attigerat: regni francor fastigii adeptus est. Et infra mensem post pris obitu. xxuus pima dca aduentus p manu uenerabilis pris Jacobi suessionensis epi uacate sedis remensi coronat' et iunuctus fuit: anno uidel; ab incarnatōe dni .M. cc. uicesimo serto. Qui siue igenuitatis

18 Henry VI presented by St Louis to the Virgin and Child

This deluxe Psalter has been both a French and an English royal book. It is suitably grand – almost every page is ornamented with a border of gold ivy leaves, and it is decorated by a series of large illustrations in the most fashionable style of the period. These paintings include six of a young boy engaged in devout conversation with the Virgin and Christ. At the beginning of Psalm 26, shown here, the boy is supported by St Louis; in another he is supported by St Catherine.

Wearing a crown and accompanied by the arms of England and France, this prince is often identified as the young Henry VI (r. 1422–61). However, the arms of England are a later addition. Given his apparent age, royal status and attendance by St Louis, it is likely that this boy is in fact the Dauphin Louis, Duke of Guyenne (b. 1397, d. 1415). In around 1405–10 Louis's mother, Isabel of Bavaria, is recorded as having devotional manuscripts made for her other children. This opulent book may also have been commissioned by the Queen as a very personalised devotional book for her young son.

The circumstances and timing of the modification of the arms (which was accompanied by the addition of even more illustrations) is unclear. One possibility is that the Psalter was acquired by Louis's sister, Catherine of France, who married Henry V in 1420. Perhaps Catherine had the luxurious book modified so that her own young son, Henry VI, could see himself in the images of the devout prince included within it.

Psalter of Henry VI
Paris, *c.* 1405–10 (with later additions)
195 x 140 mm
British Library, Cotton Domitian A. xvii, f. 50

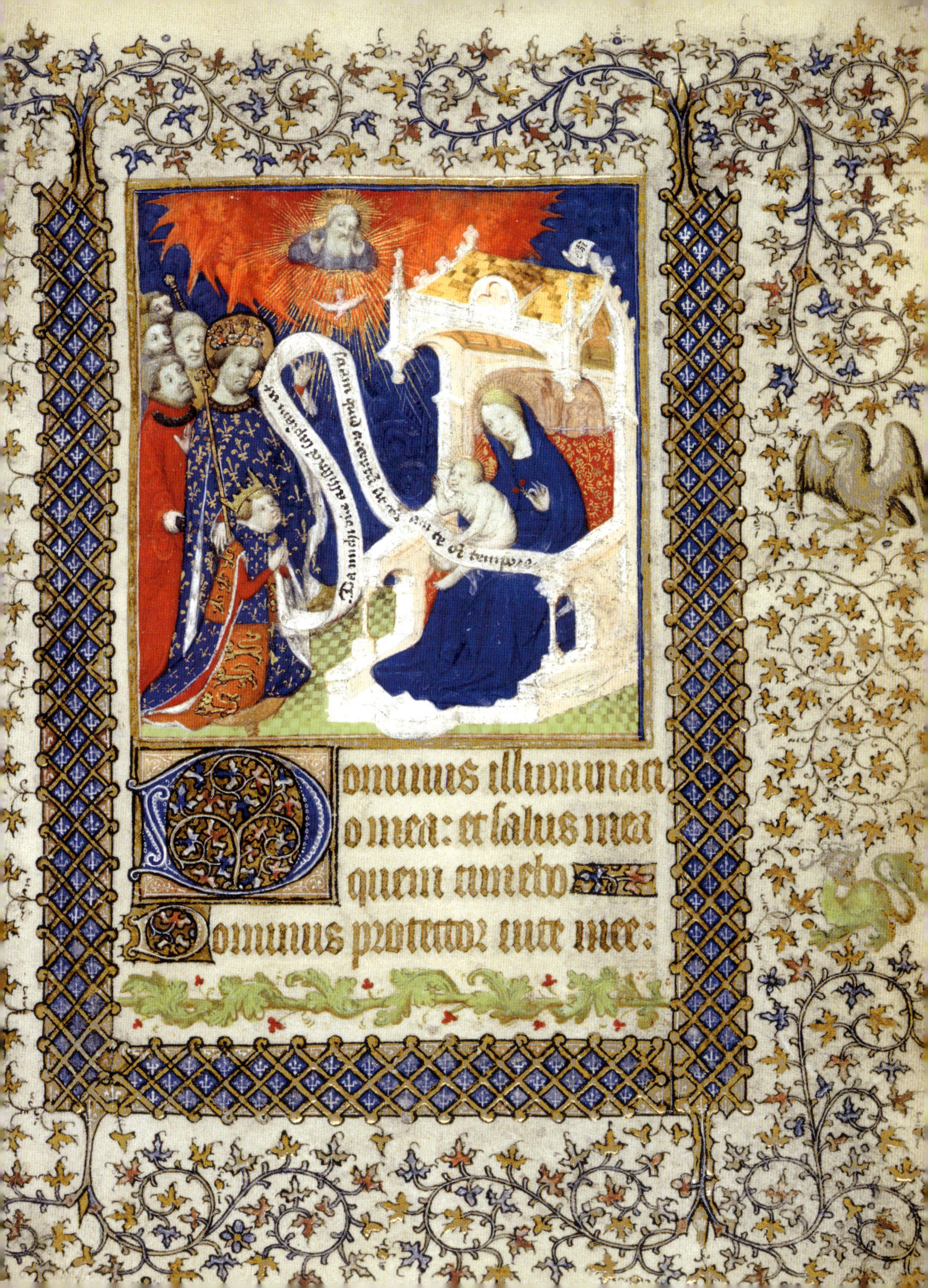

Dominus illumina-
tio mea: et salus mea
quem timebo.
Dominus protector vite mee:

19 Elkanah and his wives

At a massive 630 mm tall, this 'Great Bible' is the largest book in the exhibition, and one of the biggest manuscripts in the Old Royal library and the British Library. It is also the only manuscript in the Royal collection associated with Henry IV. Its title of the 'Great' or 'Big' Bible comes from a reference in an inventory made of books at Richmond Palace in 1535, which refers to a *Biblia magna* (Great or Big Bible), and a reference to a *Biblia magna* in Henry V's will as a Bible that had been owned by his father, Henry IV. Its huge size may indicate that it was used for readings in the royal chapel, rather than as a Bible for private study.

The Great Bible is also one of a very few extensively illustrated English biblical manuscripts to survive from the late Middle Ages. Each book opens with a historiated (or pictorial) initial and the prologues to biblical books include images of St Jerome, the translator of the Bible into Latin. For example, at the beginning of 1 Kings (1 Samuel in modern Protestant Bibles) Elkanah appears at an altar with his two wives: the childless Hannah kneels nearest the priest, while the fertile Peninah stands next to Elkanah with a line of children behind her.

The 'Great Bible'
London, *c.* 1410–15
630 x 430 mm
British Library, Royal 1 E. ix, f. 64 (detail)

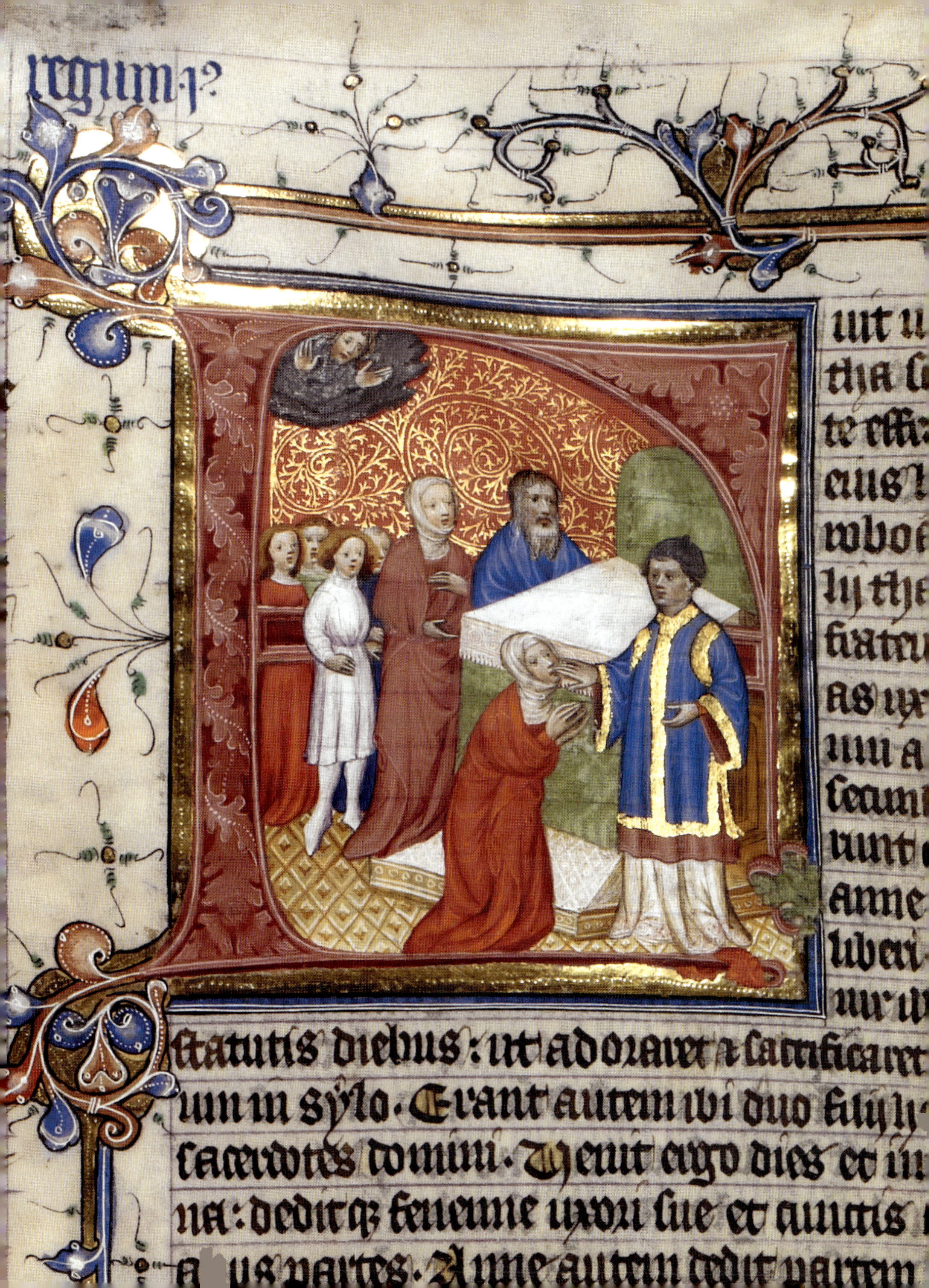

statutis diebus: ut adoraret a sacrificaret
um in sylo. Erant autem ibi duo filij h[eli]
sacerdotes domini. Venit ergo dies et im
na: deditq; fenenne uxori sue et cunctis
a us partes. Anne autem dedit partem

20 King Solomon instructing his son

More than one hundred copies of the *Bible historiale* survive. Many, like this one and no. 14, were illuminated by the finest artists of the period, befitting their status as deluxe books. Indeed, some scholars translate the title of the work as a 'historiated' (illustrated) Bible, rather than as a history Bible. The text itself was somewhat mutable. Originally only the historical books of the Bible, abridged versions of Job and Proverbs, and a combined Gospels were included. However, in the fourteenth century other biblical texts were added to make the *Bible historiale* closer to a French version of the Latin Bible, the Vulgate. The present manuscript is unique in that it includes several apocryphal stories such as a Life of Judas and of Pilate, apparently translated by Guyart des Moulins, but not included in any other known copy of the text.

The text was copied by an Augustinian friar, Thomas du Val, of Clairefontaine Abbey in the diocese of Chartres, who records that he finished the work in 1411, but he did not indicate its intended recipient. Given the extraordinary richness of its illumination, it would not be surprising if this was a royal book. Here Solomon is shown as a magnificent and imposing figure, crowned, richly dressed and holding the sceptre of power. The smaller figurer half kneeling before him is his son Rehoboam, whom Solomon is instructing, arm outstretched, presumably with the proverbs that follow: 'that men may know wisdom and instruction' (Proverbs 1:1). The beginning of the first volume (pictured overleaf) features a stunning image of God as Creator against a background of red and blue angels.

Bible historiale
Clairefontaine and Paris, 1411
445 x 340 mm
British Library, Royal 19 D. iii, vol. 2, f. 289; overleaf, vol. 1, ff. 2v–3

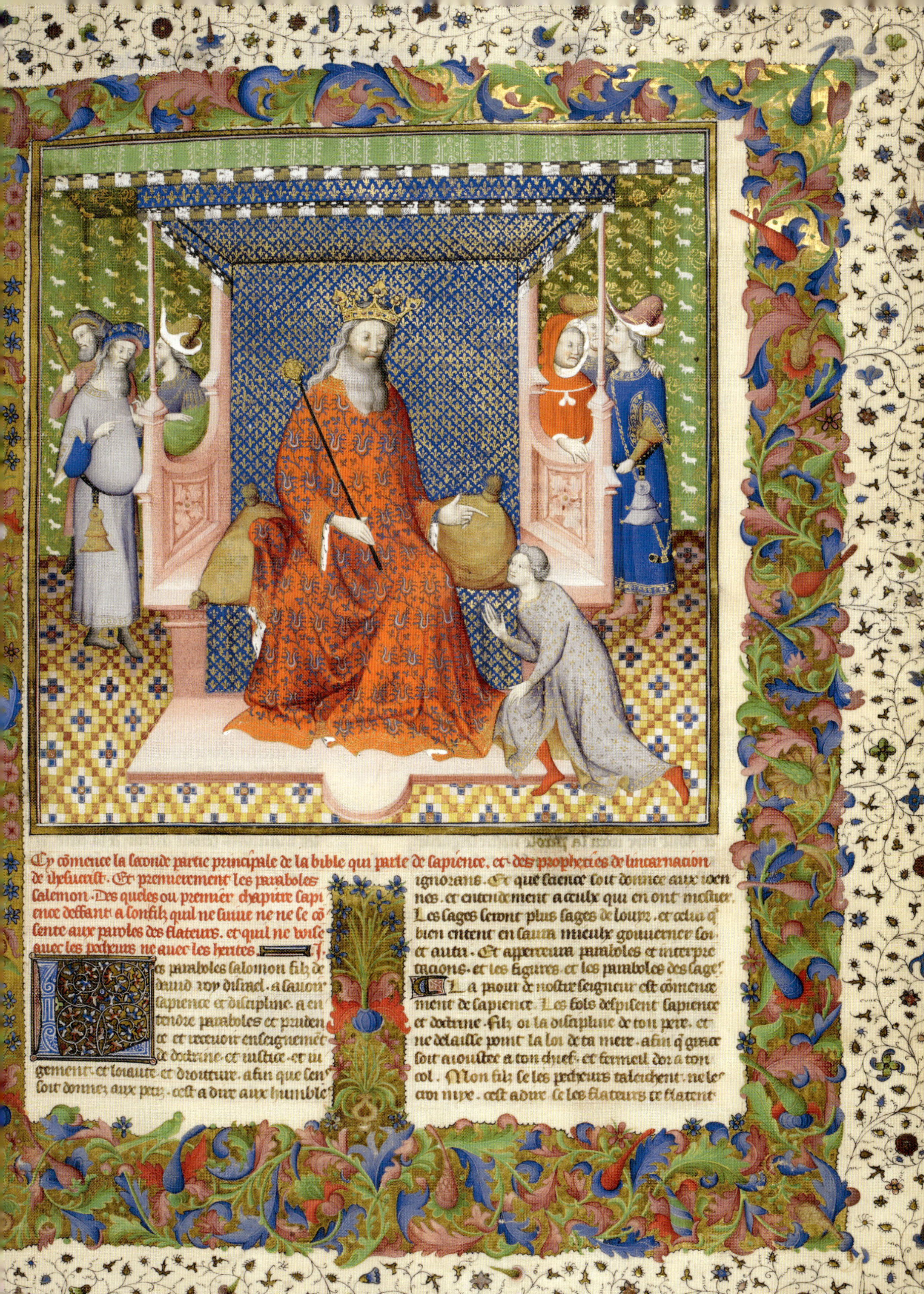

Cy comence la seconde partie principale de la bible qui parle de sapience, et des propheties de lincarnacion
de ihesucrist. Et premierement les paraboles
Salemon. Des queles ou premier chapitre sapi
ence deffant a sonfilz, quil ne suiue ne ne se co(n)
sente aux paroles des flateurs. et quil ne voise
auec les pecheurs ne auec les heretes. ·J·

[L]es paraboles salomon filz de
dauid roy disrael. a sauoir
sapience et discipline. a en
tendre paraboles et pruden
ce et receuoir enseignemet
de doctrine et iustice. et iu
gement. et loiaute et droiture. afin que sens
soit donnez aux petiz. cest a dire aux humbles
ignorans. Et que science soit donnee aux ioen
nes. et entendement a ceulx qui en ont mestier.
Les sages seront plus sages de loure. et celui q
bien entent en saura mieulx gouuerner soi
et autri. Et apercewra paraboles et interpre
taons. et les figures. et les paraboles des sages
La paour de nostre seigneur est comence
ment de sapience. Les fols despisent sapience
et doctrine. Filz, oi la discipline de ton pere. et
ne delaisse point la loi de ta mere. afin q grace
soit aioustee a ton chief. et fermeil dor a ton
col. Mon filz se les pecheurs talenchent. ne les
croi mie. cest adire se les flateurs te flatent

et enhortement du dyable de la pome mengier. et des maudicons du serpent. et de lomme. et de la femme. · xij
C oment adam et eue furent boutez hors de paradys · xiij
E la generacion adam. et des offrandes des .ij. freres cayn et abel · xiiij
E la mort abel · xv
Es generacions cayn · xvj
E seth. et de la generacion · xvij
Es generacions adam · xviij
Es causes du deluge · xix
C oment noe entra en larche · xx
N quel aage noe entra en larche · xxj
C oment noe sacrefia a dieu apres le deluge · xxij
E lyuresse noe. et de la maudicon de cham · xxiij
C oment les filz noe furent espanduz. et de nembroth · xxiiij
E la tour babel · xxv
C oment les ydoles vindrent premierement auant · xxvj
Es generacions sem · xxvij
Es ans abraham apres la mort son [pere] · xxviij
E la victoire abraham. et coment melchisedech lui vint a lencontre · xxix
U sacrefice abraham apres ce que dieu lui ot promis hoir · xxx
C oment agar fu grosse et enceinte. et hysmael fu nez · xxxj
E la couuenance de la circoncision · xxxij
Es .iij. anges que abraham recupt · xxxiij
Es .ij. anges q alerent en sodome · xxxiiij
E la destruction de sodome · xxxv
U pechie loth · xxxvj
C oment abraham ala a abymelech le roy de gerare · xxxvij
C oment ysaac fu nez. et agar fut enchacee et boutee hors · xxxviij
U puis du serement · xxxix
C oment le mouton fu sacrefiez pour ysaac · xl
E la mort sarre · xlj
C oment abraham enuoya elyezer en mesopotanie · xlij
C oment rebecque vint a ysaac · xliij
E la mort abraham · xliiij
Ystoire du naissement des regnes · xlv
U trauail rebecque a lenfanter · xlvj
C oment esau vendi son ainsnesse · xlvij
C oment ysaac ala en gerare · xlviij
Es femmes esau · xlix
Es beneicons iacob · l

U songe iacob en mesopotamie · lj
Es deux femmes iacob · lij
Es .iiij. filz lye · liij
U naissement ioseph · liiij
Es diuerses couleurs des verges · lv
E la fuite iacob · lvj
Es dons que iacob enuoya a esau · lvij
E la luicte iacob a lange. et du change de son nom · lviij
C oment esau vint a lencontre de iaco[b] et du champ en sychem · lix
E la mort des sychimiens. et du rau[i]ssement dyne la fille iacob · lx
E la mort rachel a lenfanter son filz beniamin · lxj
E la mort ysaac · lxij
C oment ioseph fu vendu · lxiij
C oment iudas engendra phares et zaram de thamar · lxiiij
E lemprisonnement ioseph · lxv
E lexposicion des songes du bouteil[lier] et du pannetier · lxvj
E lessaussement ioseph. et du songe pharaon · lxvij
C oment les freres ioseph vindrent en egipte sanz beniamin · lxviij
C oment ioseph se fist congnoistre a ses freres · lxix
C oment israel ala en egipte · lxx
C oment ioseph ala a lencontre de son pere. et le mena au roy · lxxj
U serement que ioseph fist a son [pere] · lxxij
Es beneicons effraym et manasse les filz ioseph · lxxiij
Es beneicons des xij lignees · lxxiiij
E la mort iacob · lxxv
E la mort ioseph · lxxvj

Cy fine la table sur le liure de genesis.

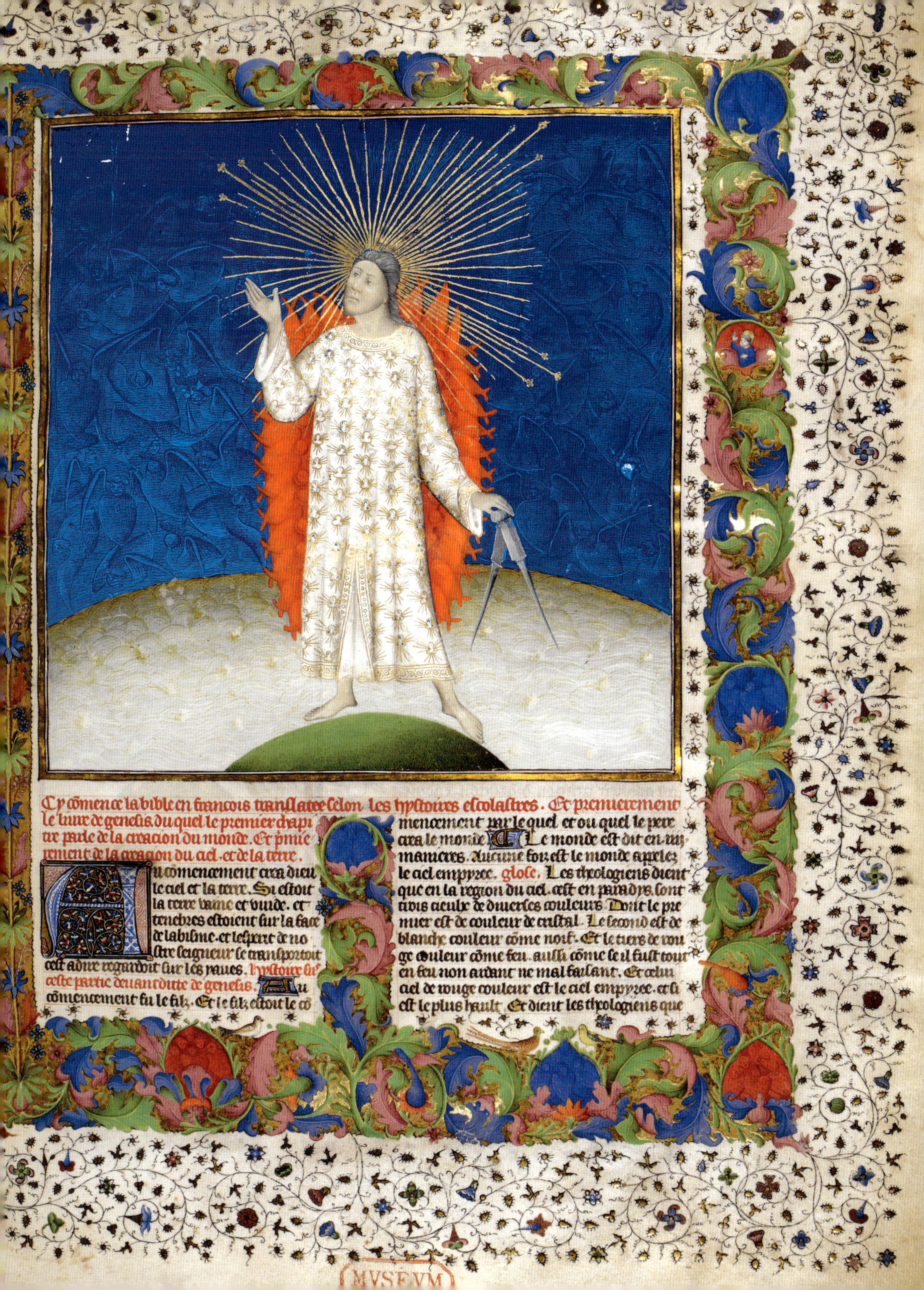

Cy commence la bible en francois translatee selon les hystoires escolastres. Et premierement
le livre de genesis du quel le premier chapi-
tre parle de la creacion du monde. Et premierement de la creacion du ciel et de la terre.

[A]u commencement crea dieu
le ciel et la terre. Si estoit
la terre vaine et vuide. et
tenebres estoient sur la face
de labisme. et lesperit de nostre seigneur se transportoit
cest adire regardoit sur les eaues. Hystoire sur
ceste partie devantdicte de genesis. [A]u
commencement fu le filz. Et le filz estoit le co-

mencement par lequel et ou quel le pere
cra le monde. Le monde est dit en au[l]-
maneres. Aucune fois est le monde appelez
le ciel empyree. glose. Les theologiens dient
que en la region du ciel cest en paradis sont
civis ceulx de diverses couleurs. Dont le premier est de couleur de cristal. Le second est de
blanche couleur come noif. Et le tiers de rouge couleur come feu. aussi come se il fust tout
en feu non ardant ne mal faisant. Et celui
ciel de rouge couleur est le ciel empyree. et li
est le plus hault. Et dient les theologiens que

21 Prince Henry in the Regement of Princes

Most of the instructional 'mirror for princes' texts (see no. 17) were composed in Latin or French. In *c.* 1411, however, the author and poet Thomas Hoccleve (b. *c.* 1367, *d.* 1426) wrote the *Regement of Princes* in English verse for Henry, Prince of Wales, who became Henry V a few years later in 1413. Hoccleve may have intended to present the text to other princes or dukes: his autograph copy includes dedication poems to Henry's younger brother John, Duke of Bedford (d. 1435), and to Henry's cousin Edward, Duke of York (b. *c.* 1373, d. 1415).

The *Regement of Princes* survives in only three illuminated copies. Scholars are divided over whether the present copy – the best preserved – was intended as a presentation copy, and, if so, for whom. A crowned, richly dressed young man (presumably the dedicatee, Prince Henry) holds a book in front of a kneeling man. In a typical donor portrait the kneeling man would be the author presenting his text. However, the arms in the initial below and others of Mowbray and Segrave later in the text indicate that the figure here may instead be John Mowbray (b. 1392, d. 1432), 2nd Duke of Norfolk and Lord Mowbray and Segrave. If so, this elegant copy may have been a gift from Prince Henry to the noble young man, rather than the presentation copy for the Prince himself.

Thomas Hoccleve, *Regement of Princes*
London *c.* 1411–13
290 x 185 mm
British Library, Arundel 38, f. 37

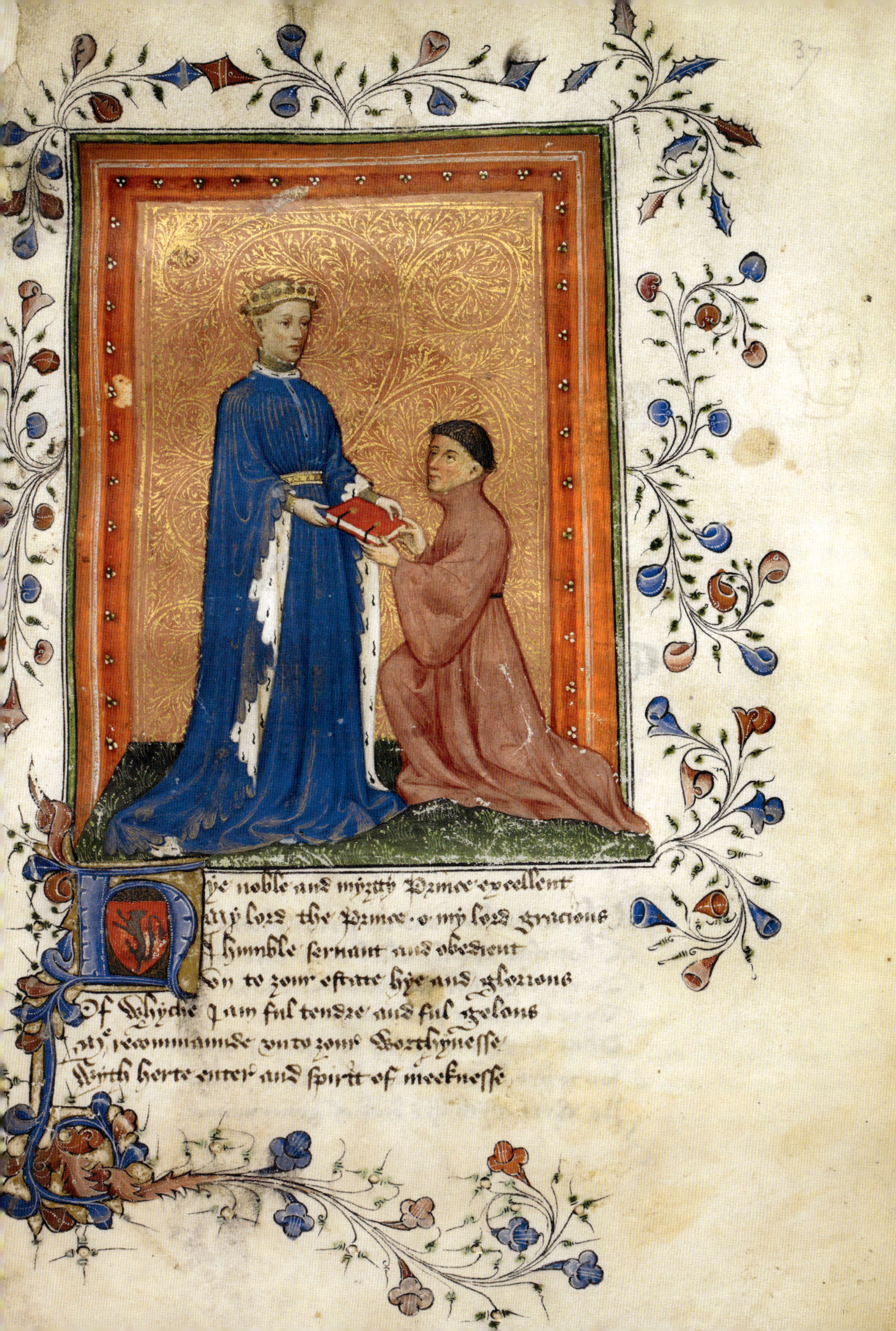

The noble and myghty Prince excellent
My lord the Prince o my lord gracious
I humble seruant and obedient
On to your estate hye and glorious
Of whyche I am ful tendre and ful gelous
ath recommaunde vnto your worthynesse
with herte enter and spirit of meeknesse

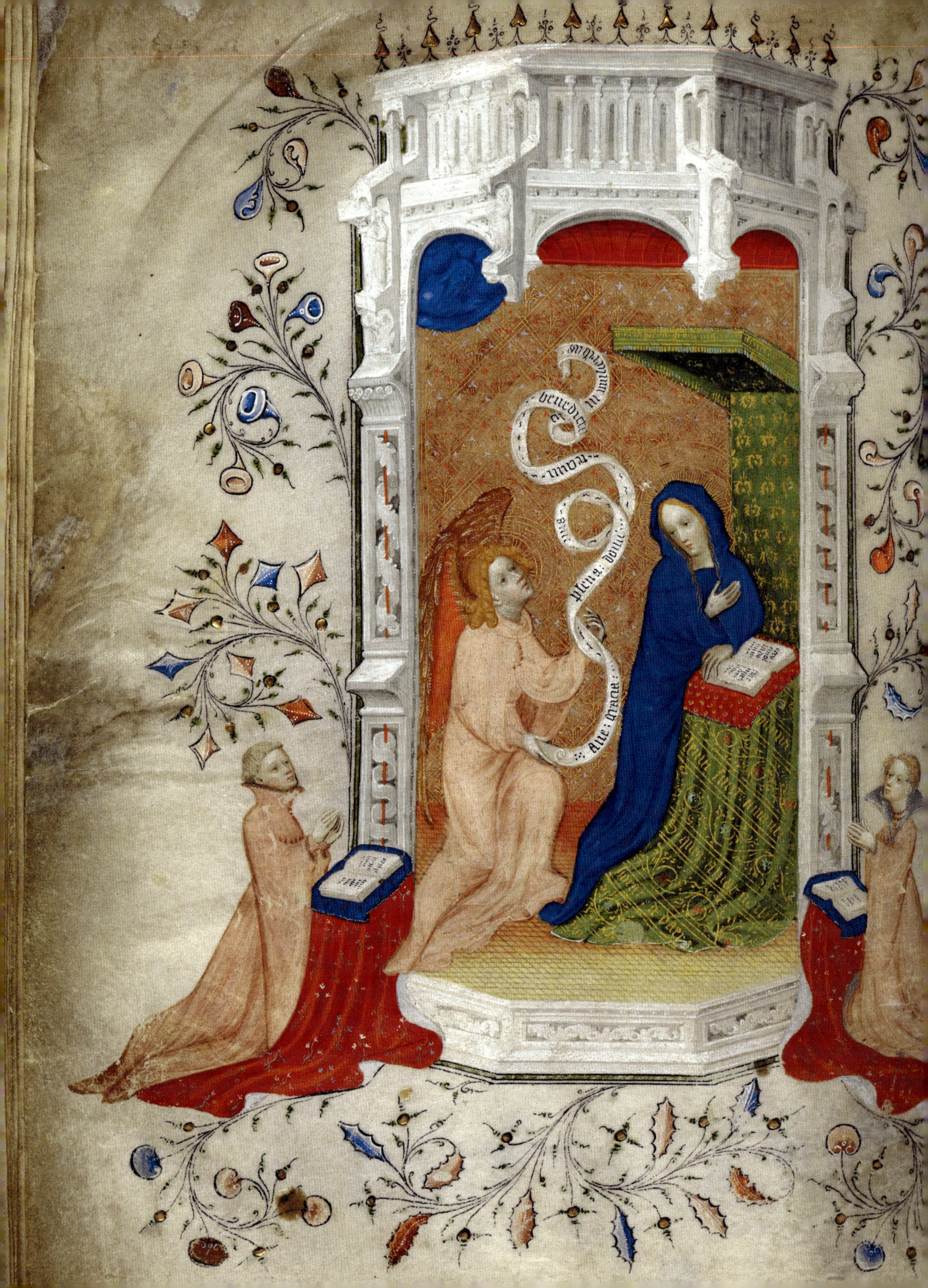

Ave maria

22 The patrons praying before the Annunciation

In the later Middle Ages the most popular type of devotional book was the Book of Hours, which contained a series of prayers to be recited at different hours of the day. These hours or times corresponded to the hours for monastic services (Matins, Lauds, Prime, Terce, Sext, None, Vespers and Compline) and, like those services, included readings from the Psalms. As in Psalters, the common lay devotional book from the earlier medieval period (compare nos. 5, 8 and 12), Books of Hours also included calendars listing saints' days and other holidays. And like luxury copies of the Psalms, elaborate Books of Hours contained painted devotional images at each of the major divisions of the text, typically events in the life of Mary, as in the *Annunciation* pictured here at the beginning of Matins.

Additions of births and deaths of family members in the calendar of this Book of Hours allow it to be identified as the prayer book of the grandmother and mother of Henry VII, Margaret Beauchamp (b. 1405/6, d. 1482), and Lady Margaret Beaufort (b. 1443, d. 1509). Margaret Beauchamp recorded the birth of her daughter Margaret, and the death of her second husband, John Beaufort, Duke of Somerset (d. 1444). In turn, Margaret Beaufort noted the birth of her son Henry, the future Henry VII, together with other significant events in his life. The images in the manuscript, including the *Annunciation* pictured, were inserts from another family prayerbook; it seems likely that the couple praying before the Virgin are John Beaufort, Earl of Somerset (d. 1410) and Margaret Holland (d. 1439), the great-grandparents of Henry VII.

Beaufort/Beauchamp Hours
Bruges and London (?), 1401–10 (the portion pictured)
British Library, Royal 2 A. xviii, f. 23v

23 Alexander the Great's exploits

Accounts of the life and exploits of Alexander the Great are known from an early period, in various versions and languages. One of the most popular of these was the tenth-century *Historia de Preliis Alexandri Magni (The History of the Battles of Alexander the Great)*. This, in turn, provided the basis for an anonymous French version, *Le Livre et la vraye hystoire du bon roy Alixandre*, usually known as the *Roman d'Alexandre en prose* or *Old French Prose Alexander Romance*, which survives in eleven known illustrated copies. As a great general, Alexander was a fitting role model for young princes and kings, particularly during the troubled period of the Hundred Years War, when military prowess was so important.

This copy of the text is a luxurious example, with eighty-six illustrations of Alexander's adventures. It was made in Paris in *c.* 1420–25, which was then the unrivalled artistic centre of Europe, and, following the Treaty of Troyes the previous year, governed by England. The artist of most of the paintings is named after this manuscript as the Master of the Royal Alexander. His skill is evident here in the image of Alexander, identifiable by his crown, fighting dragons.

It is unclear whether this book was intended from the start for a royal owner, even if the quantity and sophistication of its illustrations are certainly grand enough for one. Whoever was its original owner, by the mid-sixteenth century it had indeed found a royal home, as evidenced by the added inscription 'HR' (*Henricus Rex*) at the beginning of the book showing that the volume was in the library of the Tudor King Henry VIII.

Le Livre et la vraye hystoire du bon roy Alixandre
Paris, *c.* 1420–25
285 x 195 mm
British Library, Royal 20 B. xx, f. 49v

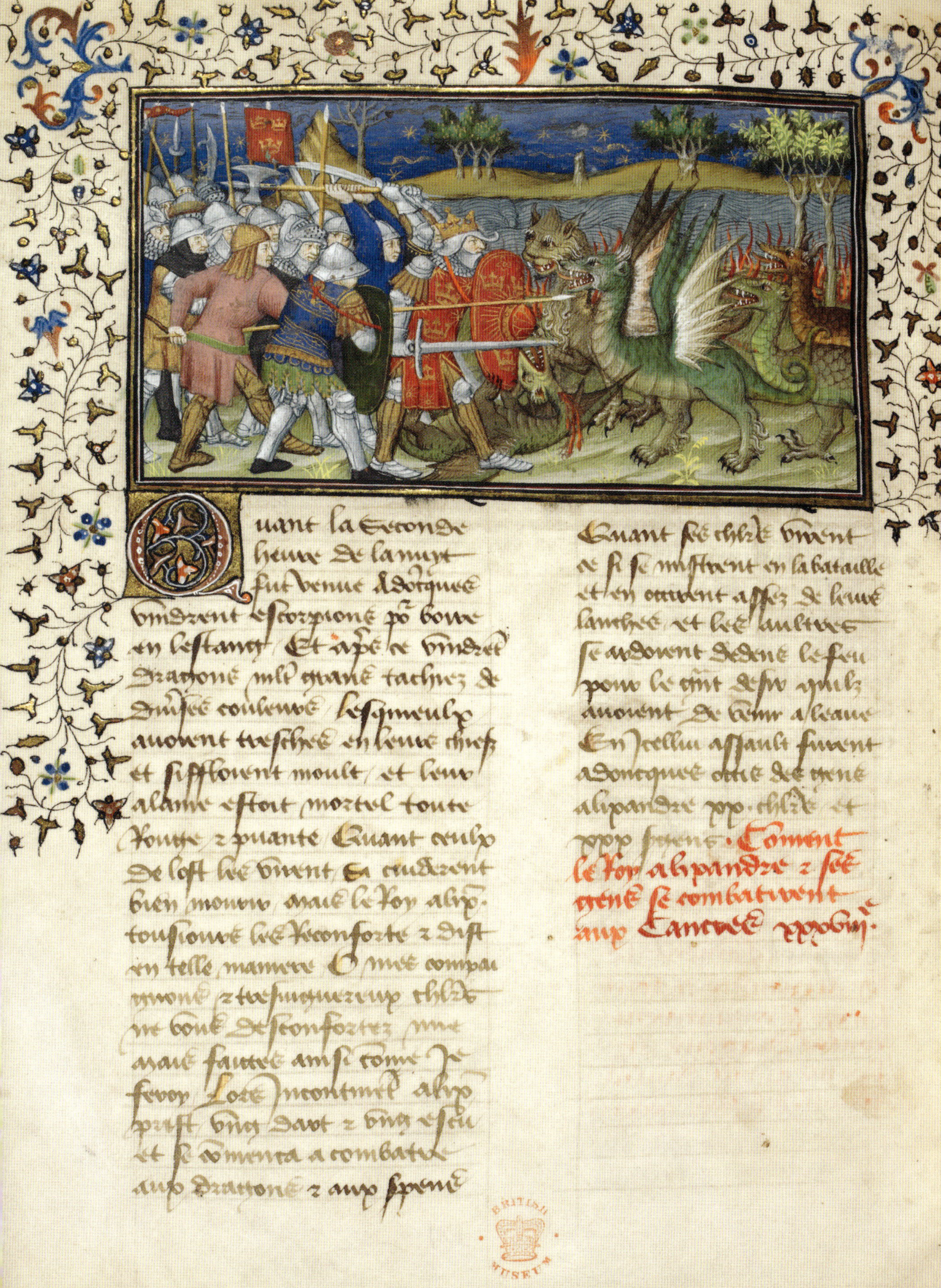

uant la seconde
heure de la nuyt
fut venue adoncques
vindrent les scorpions pour boure
en lestancy. Et apres ce vindrent
dragons mlt grans tachiez de
diuses couleurs lesqueulx
auoient tresiehies en leurs chief
et sifflouent moult, et leur
alaine estoit mortel toute
souue z puante Quant ceulx
de lost les virent ca cuiderent
bien mourus, mais le roy alix.
tousiours les reconforte z dist
en telle maniere O mes compa-
ignons z tresuaillereux chlz
ne uous desconfortez mie
mais faites ainsi comme ie
feroy. Lose Incontinent alix
prist vng dart z vng escu
et se commenta a combatre
aux dragons z aux serpens

Quant les chlz virent
ce si se misdrent en la bataille
et en occient assez de leur
lancipes et les aultres
se ardouent dedens le feu
pour le oint desir quilz
auoient de tenir aleaue.
En icellu assault furent
adoncques occis de trente
alixandre pp. chlz et
pp. serpens. Coment
le roy alixandre z ses
gens se combatirent
aux Lanctes xxobij.

24 The Crucifixion

The Hours of Elizabeth the Queen has been described as the most lavish Book
of Hours produced in fifteenth-century England. The text itself contains three
sequences of Hours: the Hours of the Virgin, the Hours of the Cross, and the
Hours of the Passion, together with a number of other devotional texts. The
illustration is particularly extensive. In addition to the full-page images before
important textual divisions, the book includes an astonishing 423 painted initials
with narrative or decorative scenes.

The manuscript is known as the Hours of the Queen because of an inscription
below the pictured image of the Crucifixion: 'Elisabeth the quene'. This appears to
be a signature of Elizabeth of York (d. 1503), daughter of Edward IV (b. 1461–83)
and wife of Henry VII (b. 1485–1509). However, the manuscript was not originally
made for her. Later in the volume is a prayer for the soul of Cecily or Cicely
(d. 1450), Duchess of Warwick, and it is likely that the book was made for a
member of her family, possibly her father, the powerful Richard Neville (b. 1400,
d. 1460), 1st Earl of Salisbury, and the nephew of Henry IV (r. 1399–1413). Thus,
this magnificent book was deemed important enough to have been passed to
senior members of the English aristocracy, in this case, ultimately the daughter,
wife, and mother of successive kings of England.

Hours of Elizabeth the Queen
London, c. 1420–30
210 x 150 mm
British Library, Additional 50001, f. 22

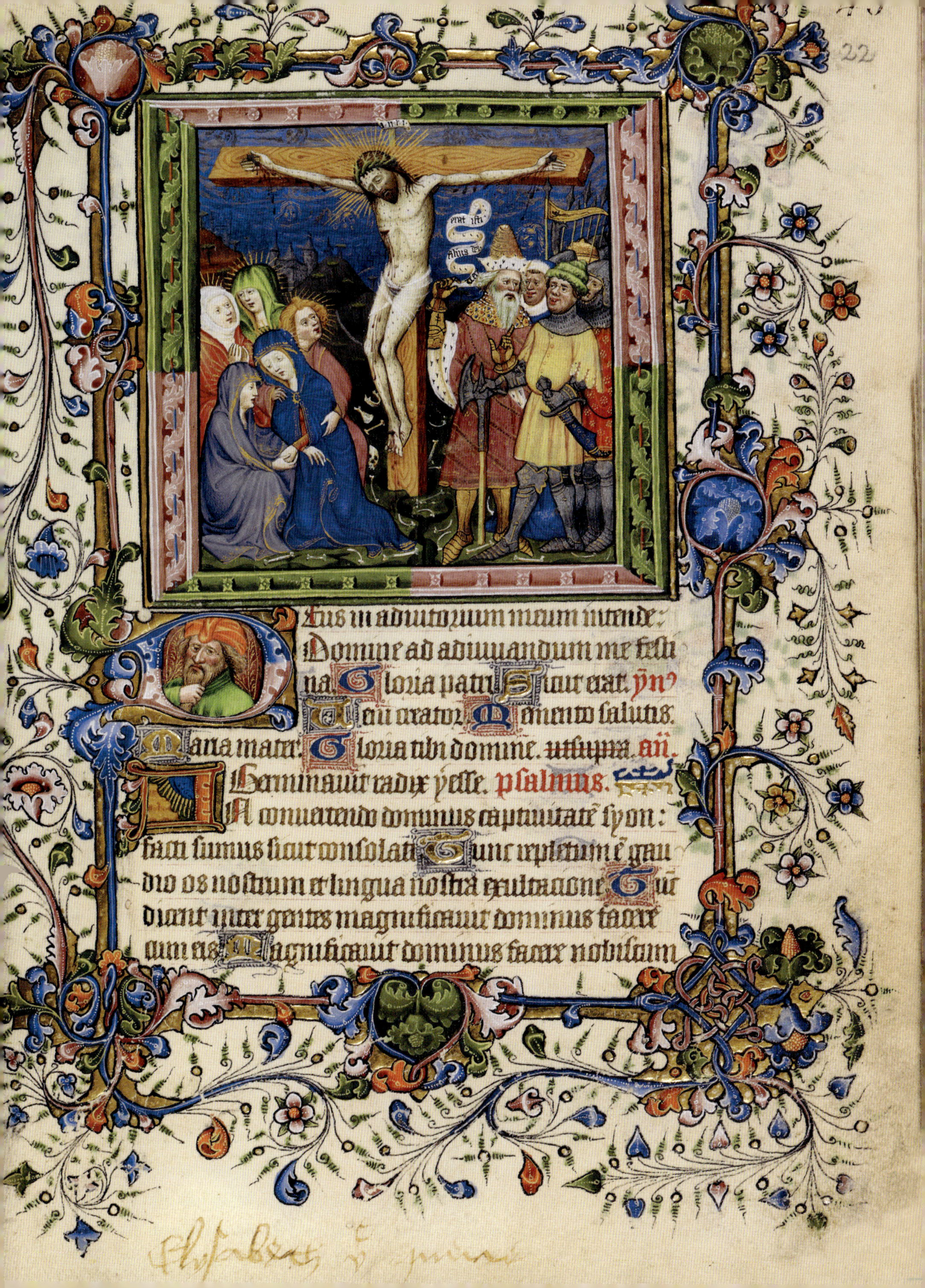

[De]us in adiutorium meum intende:
Domine ad adiuuandum me festi
na. Gloria patri. Sicut erat. ym(nus)
Teu orator. Memento salutis.
Maria mater. Gloria tibi domine. utsupra añ.
Germinauit radix yesse. psalmus.
In conuertendo dominus captiuitate(m) syon:
facti sumus sicut consolati. Tunc repletum e(st) gau
dio os nostrum et lingua nostra exultacione. Tu(n)c
dicent inter gentes magnificauit dominus facere
cum eis. Magnificauit dominus facere nobiscum

O alle men / present / or in absence
Which to seynt Edmund / haue deuocioñ
With hool herte / and dewe reuerence
Seyn this Antephne / and this Orison
Two hundred daies / ys grauntid off pardoñ
Write and registred / afforn his hooly shryne
Which for our feith / suffrede passion
Blyssyd Edmund / kyng / martir / and virgyne

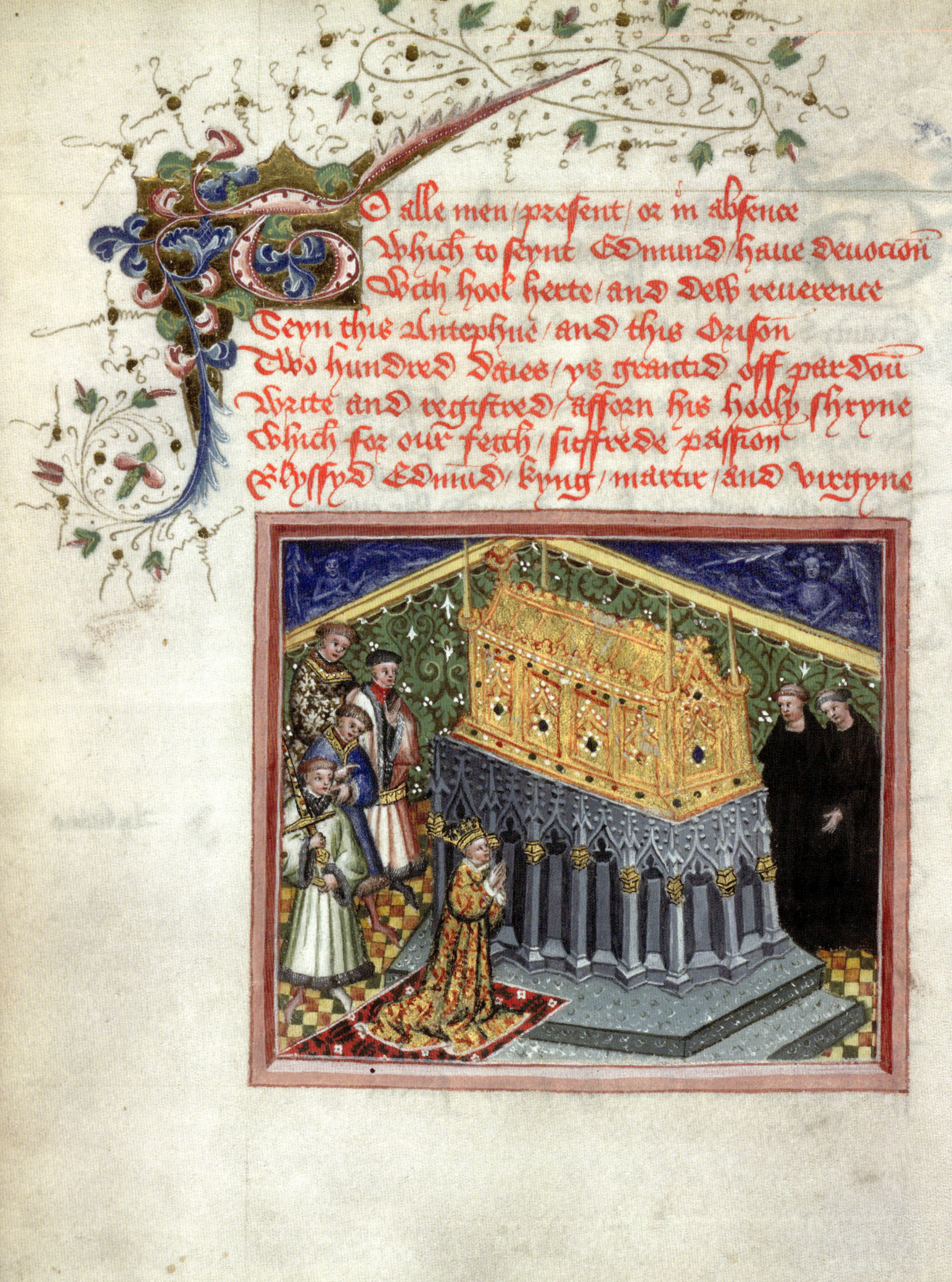

25 Henry VI before the shrine of St Edmund

In 1433 the young King Henry VI (just eleven years old) spent the period from Christmas to Easter at the abbey of Bury St Edmunds. In honour of the visit, the Abbot William Curteys commissioned an English version of the *Life* of the Abbey's patron saint from one of the Abbey's monks, the author and poet John Lydgate (d. *c.* 1451). Lydgate combined the story of Edmund's life with that of a now more obscure saint, Fremund, supposedly Edmund's nephew. This lavish and heavily illustrated copy of the text – it has 118 painted illustrations – was probably written under Lydgate's direct supervision at the Abbey as a presentation copy for the King. It is one of only twelve surviving copies of the *Life*, and the most copiously illustrated. The image pictured here is that of the kneeling King before the shrine of St Edmund at the Abbey. Although the shrine has since disappeared, in design it appears very similar to that of Edward the Confessor still standing beyond the high altar in Westminster Abbey today.

Henry VI developed a reputation for piety and poverty – qualities not necessarily viewed as appropriate for a king. He was criticised in his own time for failing to dress with appropriate magnificence, and for excessive generosity. This impressive manuscript may have been one of his gifts: a later inscription shows that it came into the possession of John Touchet (d. 1559), 8th Baron Audley, who apparently returned it to Old Royal library as a gift to Henry VIII, perhaps in thanks for the restoration of his titles in 1512.

John Lydgate, *The Lives of Saints Edmund and Fremund*
Bury St Edmunds, *c.* 1434–39
250 x 175 mm
British Library, Harley 2278, f. 4v

26 A wedding present for Margaret of Anjou and Henry VI

The Shrewsbury Book is one of the most remarkable manuscripts to have been preserved in the Old Royal library. It comprises a unique collection of fifteen texts in French that encompasses *chansons de geste*, chivalric romances and treatises on warfare and chivalry, ending with the Statutes of the Order of the Garter.

The book is perhaps even more celebrated for the two monumental images that form a frontispiece to it (pictured overleaf). On the left-hand page, the image and decorative border work together to clarify the context in which the volume had been made. From them we learn that the manuscript was a gift to Margaret of Anjou (b. 1430, d. 1482) from the renowned military commander John Talbot, 1st Earl of Shrewsbury (d. 1453). Yet, only the presentation verses record real time. Although the image represents Margaret hand-in-hand with her husband, Henry VI (r. 1422–61), and bearing the sceptre and crown of the Queen of England, Talbot's presentation probably took place before her departure from France, marriage and coronation in England in 1445. The book itself may have been made even earlier: in the accompanying verses Margaret is described as being engaged.

The image on the right-hand page (overleaf) is visually more complex, but straightforward in its aims: it presents the genealogical claim of Henry VI, visible in the lower centre of the page, to be the rightful king of France. In the diagram Henry's descent from St Louis IX (r. 1226–70) in the centre is shown both from the English line, on the right, and the French line, on the left. The French claimant to the throne, Charles VII (r. 1422–61) is, however, omitted from the line, replaced by his aunt Catherine of France (b. 1401, d. 1437), Henry VI's mother, opposite her husband Henry V (r. 1413–22) (detail opposite).

The Shrewsbury Book
Rouen, 1444–45
470 x 370 mm
British Library, Royal 15 E. vi, ff. 2v–3 (overleaf, detail opposite)

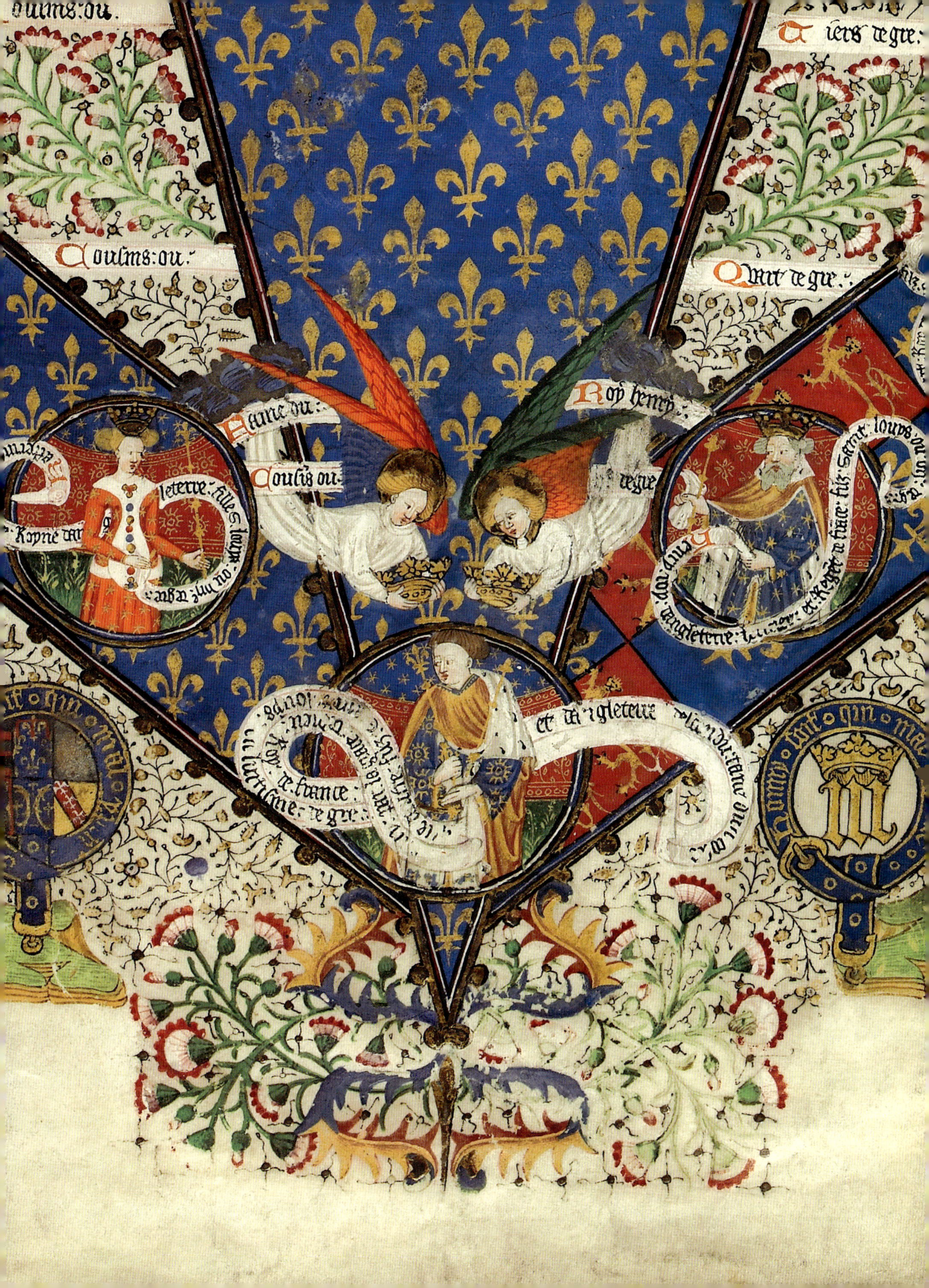

Coulins ou
Coulins ou
tiers de gre
Quart de gre
Haine ou
Coulis ou
Roy henry
de gre
Royne
gleterre filles...
Sainct louys
Roy de france et dangleterre
roy de france et de gre

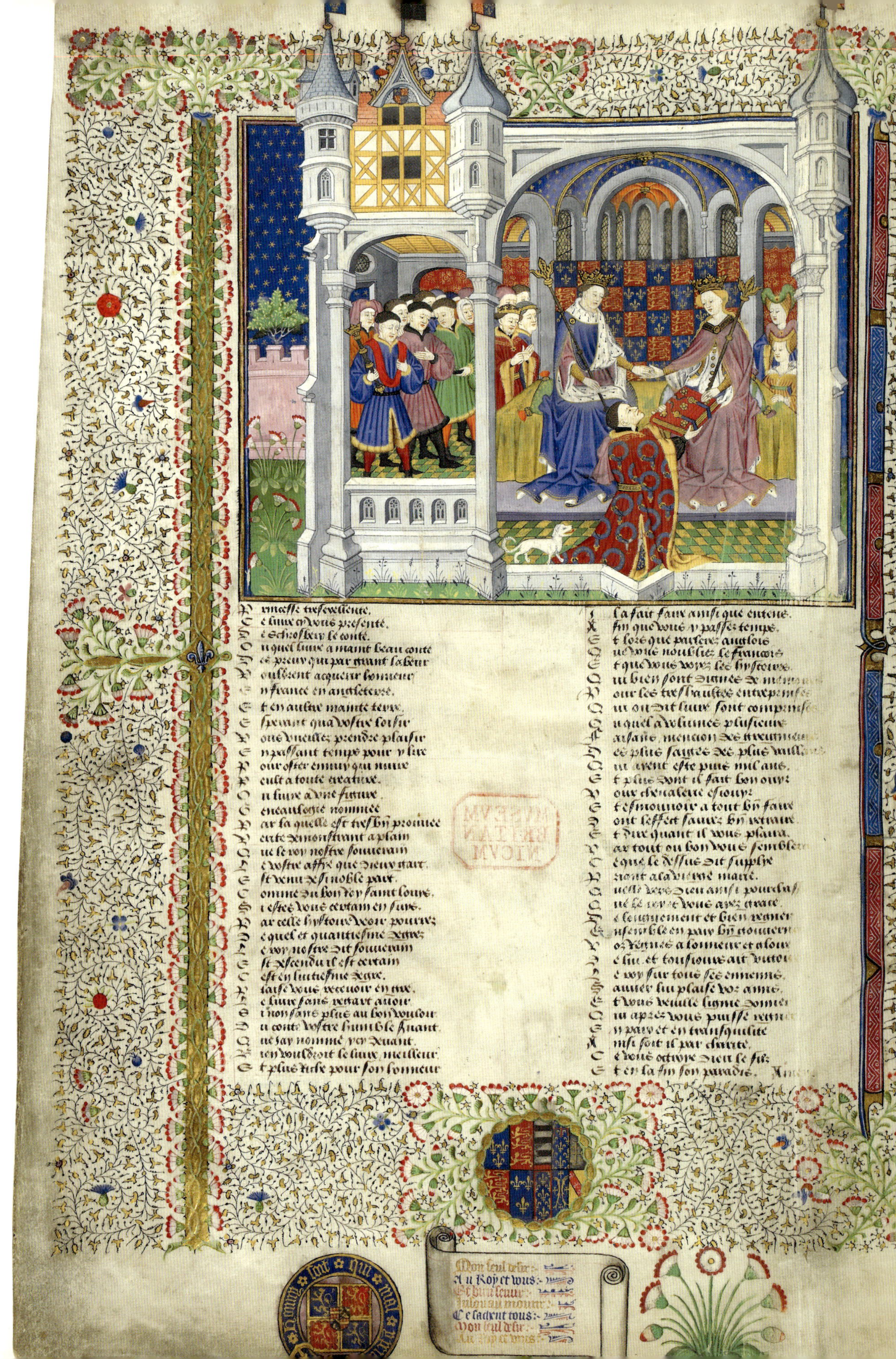

rincesse tresexcellente,
e liure on vous presente
e eschoistier le conte
n quel liure a maint beau conte
es preux qui par maint labeur
oulsirent acquerir bonneur
n france en angleterre.
t en aultre mainte terre
sceant qua vostre loisir
ous vueillez prendre plaisir
n passant temps pour y lire
our oster ennuy qui nuire
eult a toute creature.
n liure a vne future,
encauseoie nommee
ar sa quelle est tresbn prouvee
erite demonstrant a plain
ue le roy nostre souverain
e vostre affin que dieu y tait
st venu de si noble part.
omme du bon roy saint louys,
i estes vous certain en suys.
ar celle histoire veoir pourrez
e quel et quantiesme degrez
e roy nostre dit souverain
st descendu il est certain
est en huitiesme degre.
laise vous recevoir en gre,
e liure sans rettart avoir
t non sans plus au bon vouloir
u conte vostre humble suant
ue say nomme cy devant
en vouldroit le liure meilleur
t plus riche pour son honneur

la fait faux ainsi que entens.
fin que vous y passez temps,
t lors que parlerez anglois
ue vous noublies le francois
t que vous voyez les histoires
ui bien sont dignes de memoire
our les treshaultes entreprises
ui on dit leur sont comprinses
uquel a volunte plusieur
affans, mencion des travailleurs
es plus sayges des plus vaillans
ui eurent este puis mil ans.
t plus sont il fait bon ouyr
our chevalerie esiouyr
t esmouuoir a tout bn faire
ont leffect sauur bn extraire
t puis quant il vous plaira,
ar tout ou bon vous semblera
eque le dessus dit supplie
ment a la vierge marie,
uelle vers dieu ainsi pourclas
ue le roy de vous ayez grace
e longuement et bien regner
nsemble en paix bn gouverner
os regnes a lonneur et alour
e lui et tousiours ait victoire
e roy sur tous ses ennemis
auuer lui plaise voz amis,
t vous veuille ligne donner
ui apres vous puisse regner
n paix et en tranquilite.
nsi soit il par charite.
e vous octroye dieu le fiz
t en la fin son paradis. Amen.

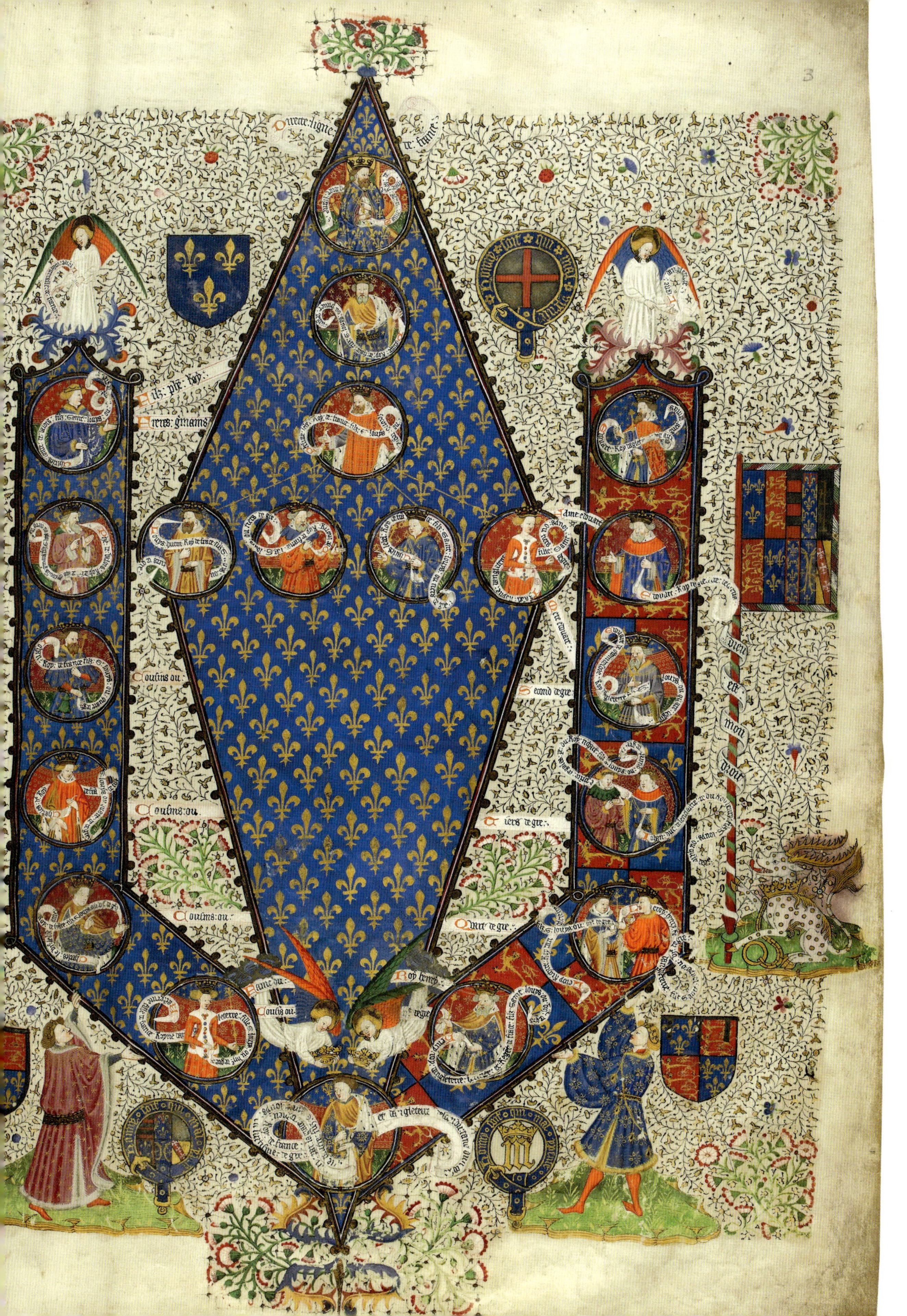

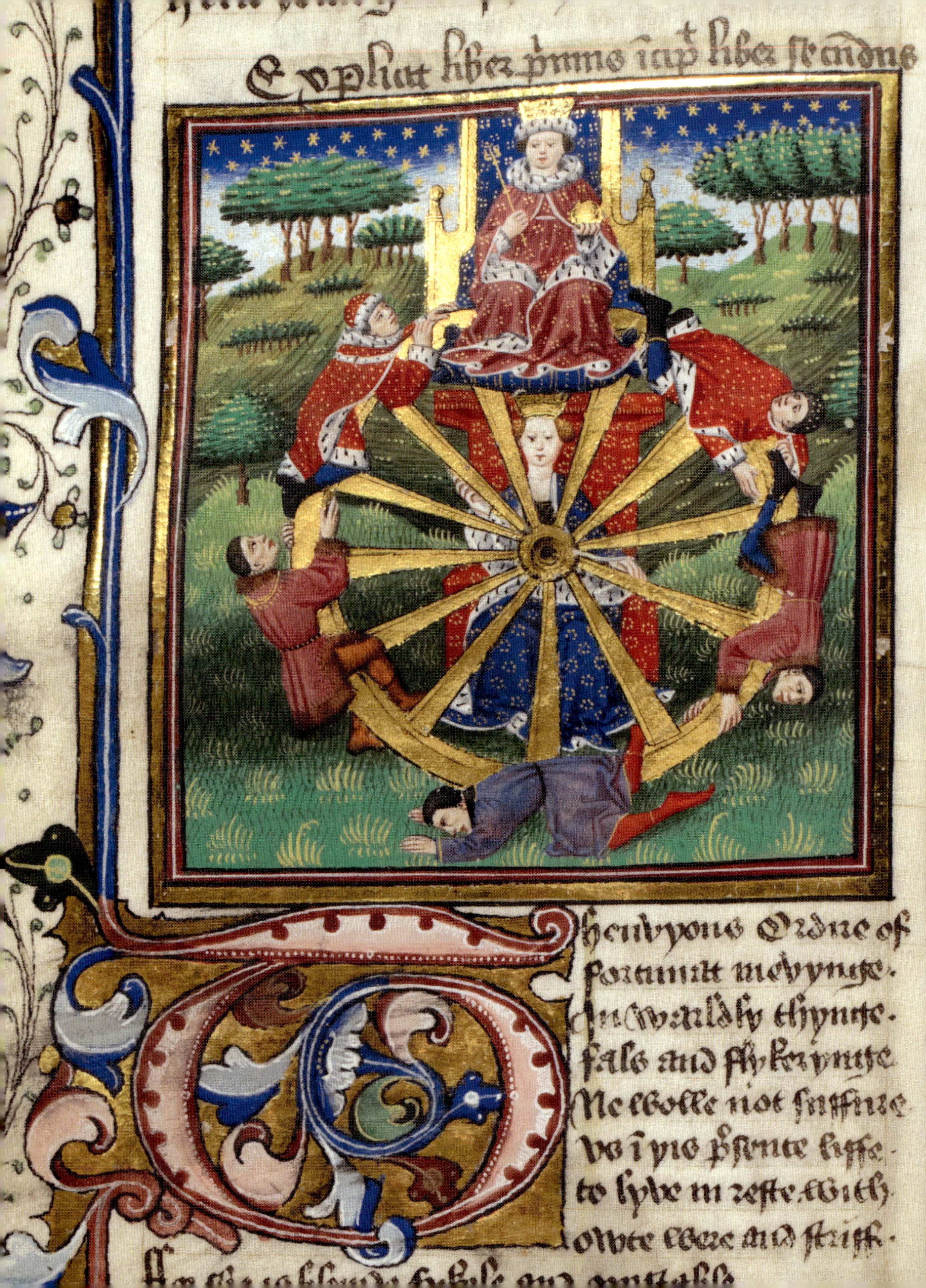

Heir vpon this Ordne of
fortunit mevynge.
In worldly thynge.
fals and flykerynge.
Ne wolle not suffice
vs in this psente liffe.
to lyve in reste. with
oute were and striffe.

27 The Wheel of Fortune

Like the characters in the mirror for princes texts (see nos. 17 and 21), historical figures also served as exemplars for princes and other nobles. The legend of Troy was particularly popular because all European royalty traced their descent from Trojan heroes. In the fifteenth century the poet John Lydgate (d. *c.* 1451) provided an English version of these stories, which had previously circulated in French and Latin.

The present manuscript must have been commissioned by Sir William Herbert (d. 1469) and his wife Anne Devereux (d. *c.* 1486), who are depicted in a large image with their arms and motto, kneeling before an enthroned king. It is likely, therefore, that the Herberts presented the copy to a king, although opinions differ on whether this was the Yorkist Edward IV (r. 1461–83) or the Lancastrian Henry VI (r. 1422–61, d. 1471). Lydgate himself was a Lancastrian supporter, as is clear from the text of his prologue, which praises Henry V. The inclusion of this prologue makes it more likely that this book was intended as a gift to Henry's son.

The illustration pictured is unique amongst the seven extant illuminated copies of the Troy Book. It reminds the reader of the fragility of power, a lesson appropriate to either of the possible royal recipients. A crowned king sits atop a gold wheel being turned by a crowned personification of Fortune, who topples mercilessly other richly dressed figures – a fitting metaphor for the shifting fortunes of the Lancastrian and Yorkist kings.

John Lydgate, *Troy Book* and *Siege of Thebes*, with verses by William Cornish, John Skelton, William Peeris and others
395 x 280 mm
England, *c.* 1457 (with later additional illustrations)
British Library, Royal 18 D. ii, f. 30v (detail)

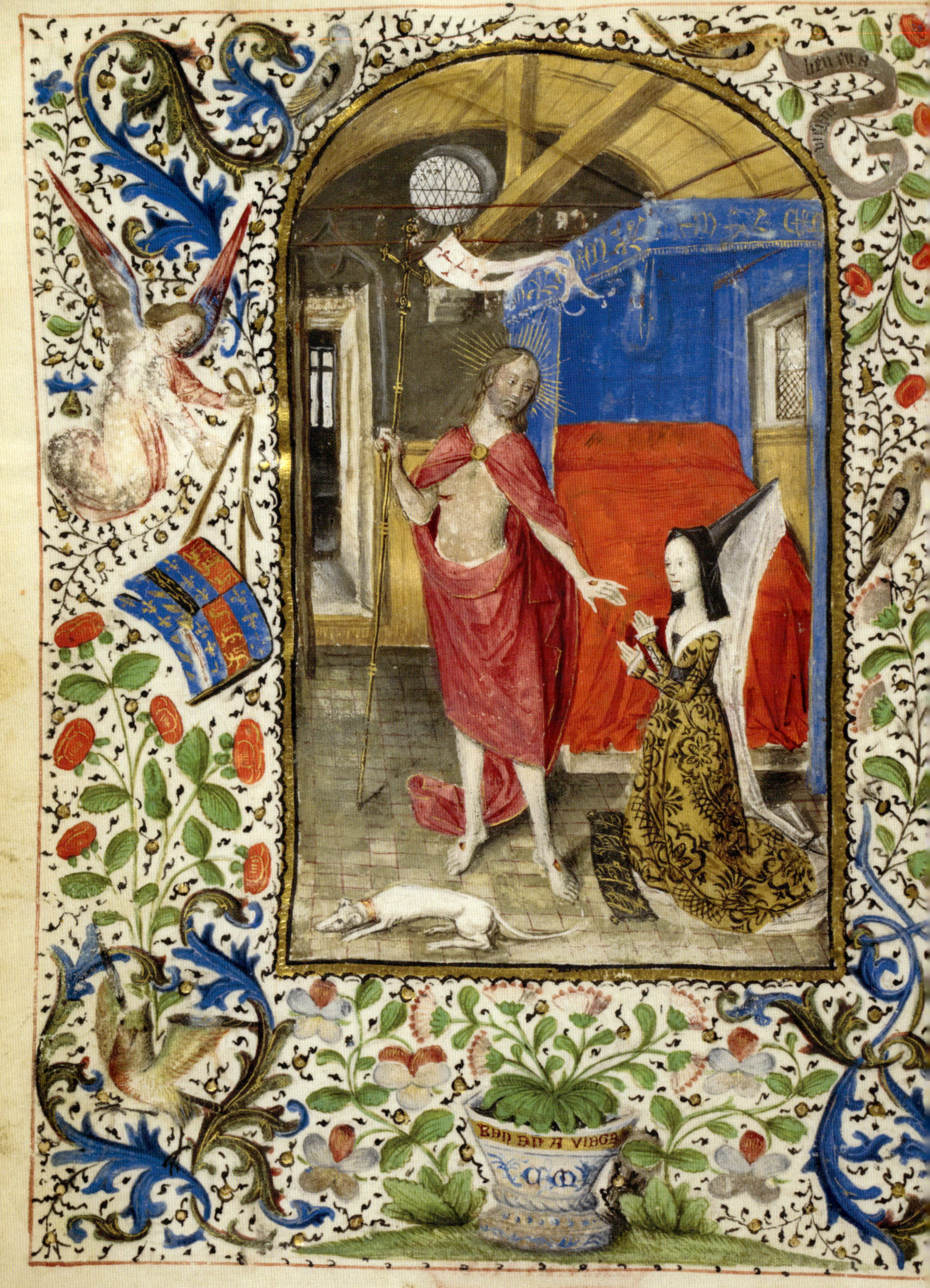
ben ela
ben ela
ban ba a vidoa

28 Margaret of York in dialogue with the resurrected Christ

The present manuscript is a unique copy of a devotional text written for Margaret of York (b. 1446, d. 1503), the sister of Edward IV. Her marriage in 1468 to Charles the Bold (r. 1467–1477), Duke of Burgundy, one of the richest men in Europe, was one of the most stylish ceremonies of the century. The artistic and other fashions of the Burgundian court proved highly influential in the Yorkist court. This work was undertaken by Margaret's almoner, or chaplain, Nicolas Finet, perhaps commissioned by someone at the Burgundian court to help shape Margaret's new life as Duchess. The result was the *Dialogue de la duchesse de Bourgogne à Jésus Christ*, a deeply personalised text in which Margaret receives instruction directly from Christ and is urged to contemplate his living presence.

The work is personalised still further with an image of the Duchess herself in her private chamber experiencing a vision of Christ. In composition this image is redolent of familiar *Noli me tangere* scenes of Christ appearing to Mary Magdalene; perhaps the Duchess was being encouraged to emulate the piety of other holy women such as the Magdalene. Margaret's arms as Duchess of Burgundy appear in the lower border, together with her device *Ben en aviegne* (May good come of it) and her initial entwined with that of her husband Charles's. Nevertheless, this manuscript may never have been part of a royal or ducal library. Margaret gave the manuscript to her friend and lady-in-waiting Jeanne de Hallewin (d. 1529), Lady of Wassenaer, and recorded this gift in an autograph dedication at the end of the volume.

Nicolas Finet, *Dialogue de la duchesse de Bourgogne à Jésus Christ*
Brussels, *c.* 1468
220 x 140 mm
British Library, Additional 7970, f. 1v

29 Charles the Bold receiving Vasco da Lucena's text

In the prologue to *Les Fais d'Alexandre le grant* the Burgundian courtier Vasco da Lucena sought to prepare his readers for a distinctive aspect of his account of Alexander. In contrast to the 'fables made up by men ignorant of the nature of things … the present history is much more useful. For it tells us how in reality Alexander conquered the whole of the East and how in our day a ruler could really achieve such conquests.' By this means Vasco da Lucena clearly signalled how his account of the deeds of Alexander the Great would differ from the centuries-old tradition of the Romance of Alexander (compare no. 23). Completed in 1468 and dedicated to Charles the Bold, Duke of Burgundy (r. 1467–77), Vasco's text forms a landmark in humanistic writing produced in northern Europe. The author's presentation of the book to Charles is pictured here.

This radical approach proved notably popular, with thirty-four copies of Vasco's text surviving, all of which were made within the translator's lifetime by professional book producers in northern Europe, most in the southern Netherlands or what is now northern France. No other Burgundian court text survives in similarly large numbers or was so frequently and extensively illustrated, or transmitted in such large numbers outside the Burgundian Netherlands. The present copy is a good example. It soon passed to Sir John Donne (d. 1503), a close associate of Edward IV (r. 1461–83), possibly during Donne's embassy to the Low Countries in 1477. It later entered the Old Royal library, perhaps as a gift from one of Donne's sons to Henry VIII.

Vasco da Lucena, *Les Fais d'Alexandre le grant* (French translation of Quintus Curtius Rufus, *Historiae Alexandri magni*)
Amiens or Bruges, 1475–80
430 x 335 mm
British Library, Royal 15 D. iv, f. 11

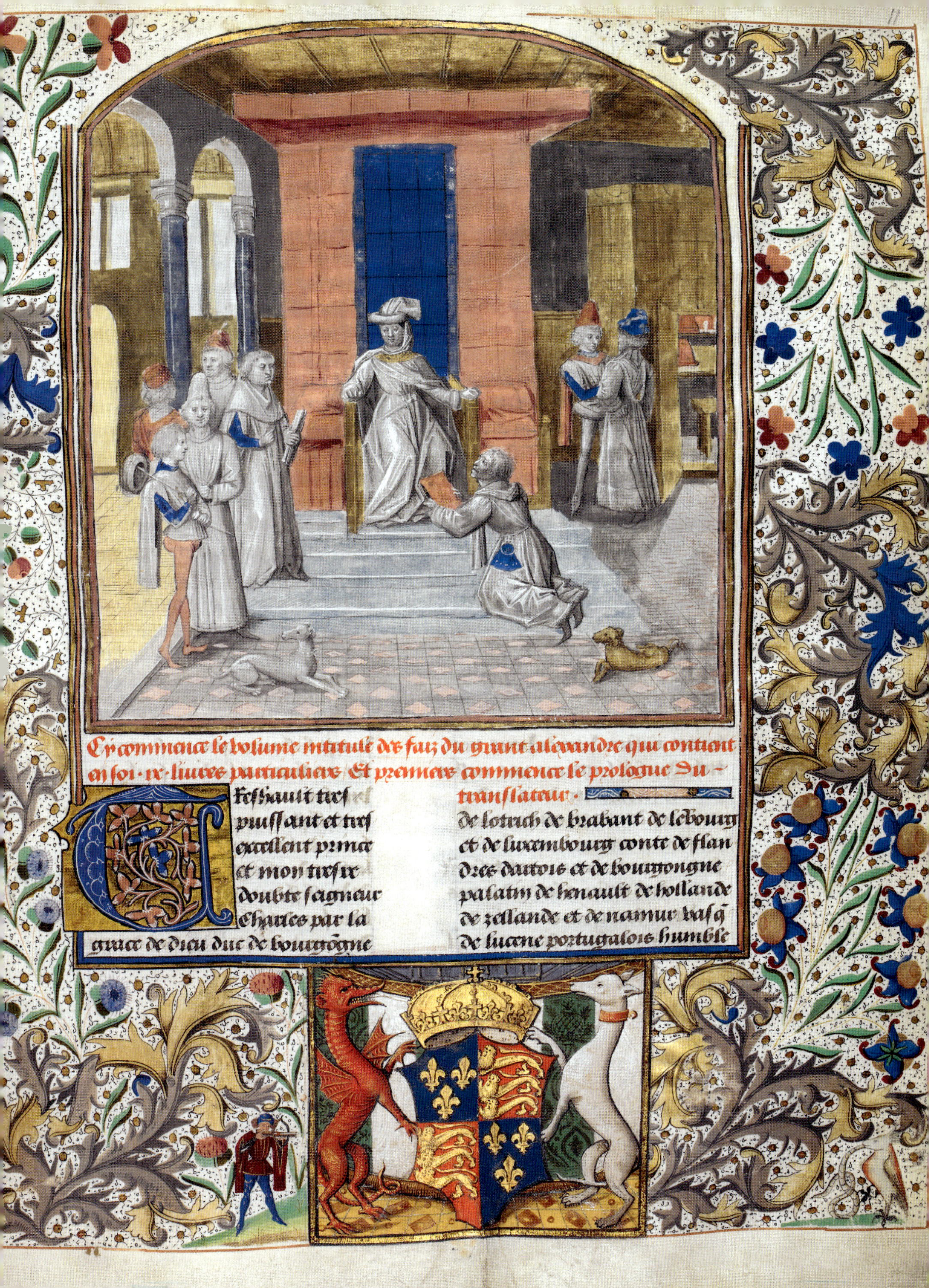

Cy commence le volume intitule des faiz du grant alexandre qui contient en soi ·ix· livres particuliers / Et premier commence le prologue du translateur ·

Tresshault tres
puissant et tres
excellent prince
et mon tresse
doubte saigneur
Charles par la
grace de dieu duc de bourgongne

de lotrich de brabant de lebourg
et de luxembourg conte de flan
dres dartois et de bourgongne
palatin de henault de hollande
de zellande et de namur vasg
de lucene portugalois humble

30 The author presenting his chronicle to Edward IV

Approaching old age and able neither to take up arms nor to undertake long journeys, Jean de Wavrin (b. *c.* 1400, d. *c.* 1472–75), Lord of Le Forestel, turned to writing to avoid idleness, 'the mother of all vices'. His subject was the history of England from legendary times to his own day. The outcome, a compilation based on other writings, was a work of monumental proportions that encompassed six huge volumes and took the last twenty-five years of Wavrin's life to complete. Although Wavrin was aware of the instructional value of historical writing, his overall approach was to provide pleasing entertainment to his fellow aristocratic readers. The present manuscript purports to be the first volume of a new edition of the *Recueil*, with a new prologue written after Wavrin's death. The new prologue's contorted and incoherent language confirms it as the product of commercial piracy. While other pirated versions of Wavrin's text are preserved, this is the only known copy containing this new prologue.

The imagery at the beginning of the prologue seems unambiguously to identify the manuscript as a commission of Edward IV. In the lower border the English royal arms are supported by Edward's lions of March, and in a large and famous portrait the King himself is depicted wearing the collar of the Order of the Golden Fleece, which he had received in 1468. Yet, the prologue and its illumination were clearly added to the volume after the rest of the manuscript had been completed, and were written by a different scribe. Thus, the present copy of the *Recueil* may not have been begun for Edward IV, but rather transferred to him at a late or later stage when his image and arms were added.

Jean de Wavrin, *Recueil des chroniques d'Engleterre*, vol. 1
Bruges, *c.* 1475
460 x 345 mm
British Library, Royal 15 E. iv, vol. 1, f. 14

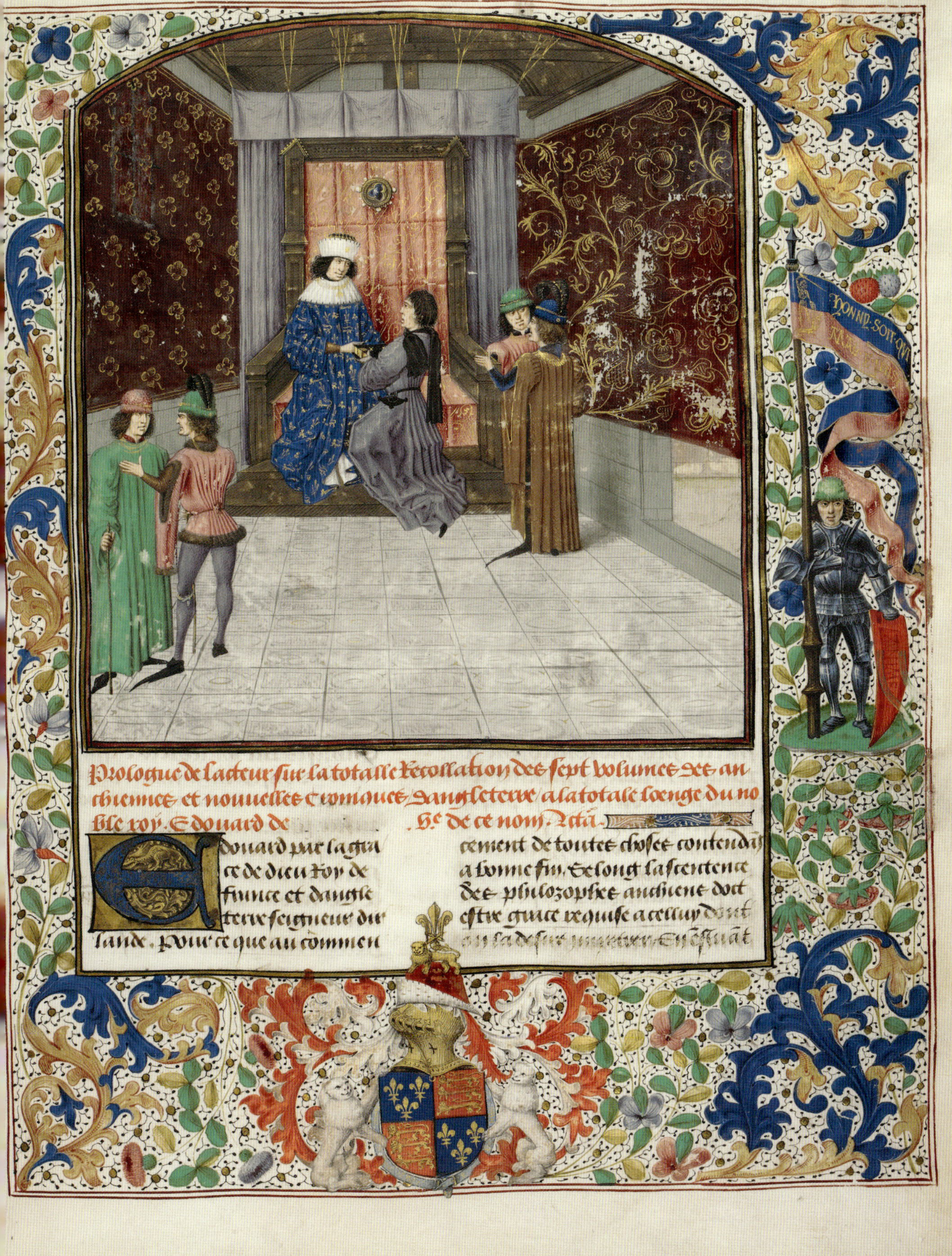

Prologue de lacteur sur la totalle recollation des sept volumes des an-
thiemies et nouuelles cromques dangleterre a la totale loenge du noble roy Edouard de   iiiie de ce nom. Actu-

Edouard par la gra-
ce de dieu roy de
france et dangle-
terre seigneur dir-
lande. Pour ce que au commencement de toutes choses contendis
a bonne fin. Selonc la sentence
des philozophes anchiens doit
estre grace requise a celluy dont
on la desir impetrer. En ensuiuat

31 The birth of Caesar, with the arms of Edward IV

Edward IV (r. 1461–83) is known as the founder of the English 'Old Royal library', because his is the first collection of illuminated manuscripts owned by a monarch to have survived as a group. Around twenty of these can be identified by the presence of his heraldic arms, often with those of his two sons, and another thirty or so can be associated with his personal library. Moreover, with only two exceptions, these books have stayed together to the present day and still form the heart of the Royal collection in the British Library.

This copy of the anonymous thirteenth-century text, the *Faits des Romains*, is characteristic of this group in that it is a large-format work of history. Edward seems to have been particularly interested in history, especially of the ancient world and Rome. His manuscripts are also very similar in format and decoration. All were ordered from the Burgundian Netherlands, a key centre of artistic production in the second half of the fifteenth century. This manuscript is the only one of the group to have an original scribal inscription at the end of the volume, stating that it was written expressly for the King, and giving the date of completion as 1479, but it is likely that the rest of the group was also made around this period. The artistic quality of the decoration in Edward's manuscripts is uniformly high, featuring large images illustrating their texts, as here with the Caesarian section birth of Julius Caesar (d. 44 BC).

La grande histoire Cesar (Faits des Romains)
Bruges, 1479
480 x 380 mm
British Library, Royal 17 F. ii, f. 9

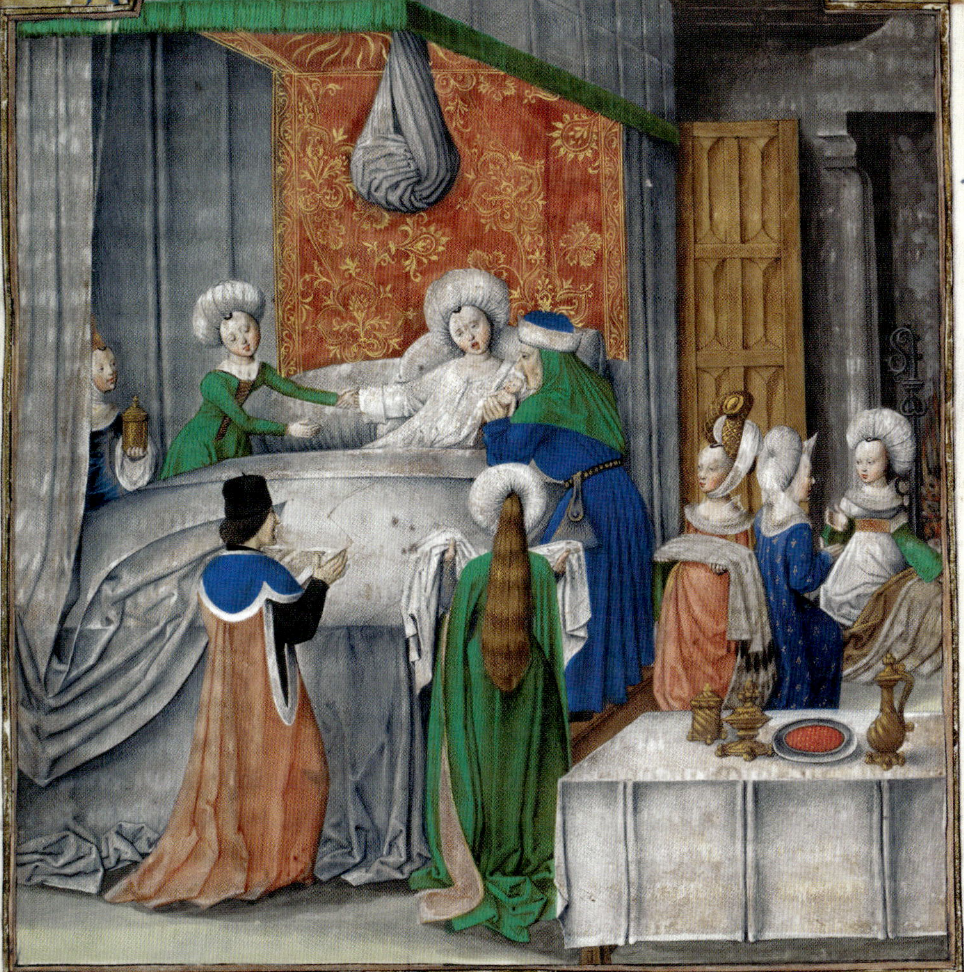

[C]hascun hôme a qui dieu a dorme raison et entendemēt se doibt pener qul ne gaste le temps en oisuete et qul ne viue comme beste qui est eudine et obeyssante a son ventre tant seulement. La vertu et la force de lhomme est en lame et ou corps ensamble. Lame doibt cōmander et le corps seruir et obeyr / Car lame a en soy lymage de dieu et la samblance pareillement et le corps est plus commun a bestialle foiblesse. Et pour ce q vault acquerre gloire il la doibt plus connoittier par richesse de sens et dauym que par richesse de force ne dauoir. La vie de lhōme est briefue mais vertu raisō

32 Protesting laws regulating sumptuous dress

To judge from the number of surviving copies, the *Facta et dicta memorabilia (Memorable Deeds and Sayings)*, written by Valerius Maximus, was the most popular Latin historical text in the Middle Ages. A French translation was begun for Charles V of France (r. 1364–80), but completed only at the beginning of the fifteenth century for Charles's younger brother, John, Duke of Berry (d. 1416). This French translation also proved extremely popular, with at least sixty-five surviving copies, many of them extensively illustrated.

One of these is this impressive two-volume set made for Edward IV (r. 1461–83). This commission was one of the several manuscripts decorated with Edward's arms and those of his sons (see also nos. 31, 33). Each of the nine books of the text features a large illustration. The first of these includes an indication of the date when it was made – 1479, the same year Edward's copy of another work of Roman history, the *Faits des Romains* (no. 31) was written, according to an inscription recorded by the scribe. Book 9 covers such themes as self-indulgence, avarice and 'haughty behaviour', so it is appropriate that the illustration for this book is of richly dressed women appearing before the tribunes Marcus Junius Brutus and his brother Publius, to protest against the *Lex Oppia*, a sumptuary law designed to prevent extravagance and luxury instituted by Gaius Oppius (first century BC), a friend of Julius Caesar's (d. 44 BC).

Simon de Hesdin and Nicolas de Gonesse, *Faits et dits mémorables des romains*
(French translation of Valerius Maximus, *Facta et dicta memorabilia*)
Bruges, 1479
480 x 340 mm
British Library, Royal 18 E. iv, f. 229

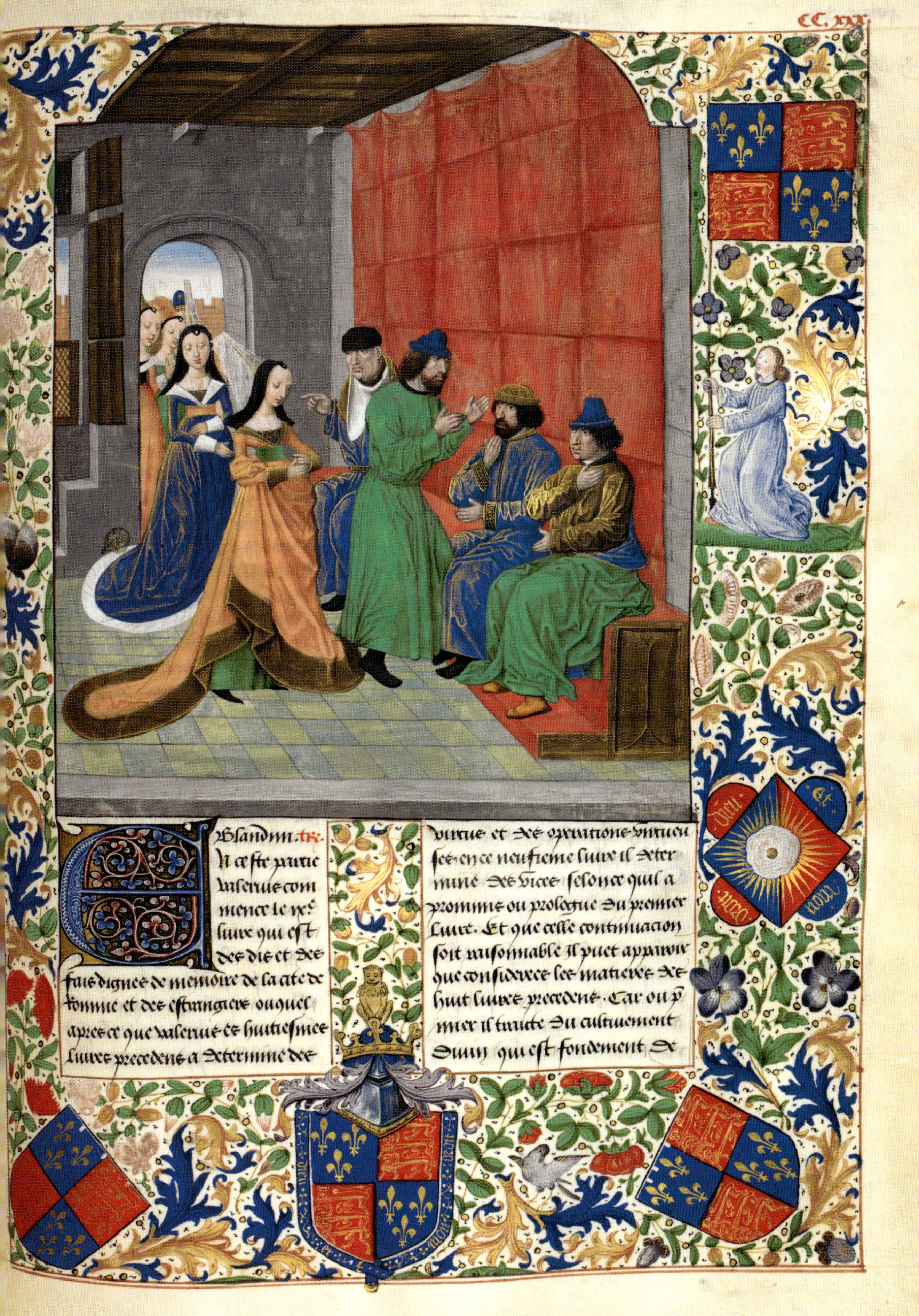

Blandin̄. tr̄.

En ceste partie Valerius commence le ix.e liure qui est des dis et des fais dignes de memoire de la cite de romme et des estrangiers ouquel apres ce que Valerius es huitiesmes liures precedens a determine des vertue et de operatione virtu set en ce neufieme liure il determine des vices selon ce quil a promys ou prologue du premier liure. Et que celle continuacion soit raisonnable Il puet apparoir que considerez les matieres de huit liures precedens. Car ou premier il traicte du cultivement divin qui est fondement de

33 Vincent of Beauvais at work in his study

The *Miroir historial* (Mirror of History) is one of a remarkable sequence of translations that were undertaken in the second quarter of the fourteenth century by a member of the order of the Knights Hospitaller, Jean de Vignay (b. *c.* 1283). Through it de Vignay opened up to an aristocratic readership part of Vincent of Beauvais's monumental work of Latin scholarship, the *Speculum maius,* and introduced them to a wealth of encyclopaedic knowledge set within a historical framework. The broad historical period of the *Miroir* begins with the Creation and continues to Vincent's own times. The first part alone includes such topics as the Marvels of the East, Greek and Roman history and legend, and the Bible.

The present manuscript was owned by Edward IV, as is evident from the Yorkist badge of the *rose-en-soleil* and the English royal arms in the right border, together with Edward's arms and those of his sons in the lower border (compare nos. 31 and 32). These features conform to a template that was drawn up for the use of the Netherlandish artists who illuminated Edward's manuscripts. Heraldic accuracy was sacrificed for symmetry of design in the lower border: the quarters of the royal arms in the left-hand shield are inverted.

The well-known image at the beginning of the volume shows the Dominican author of the original Latin text, Vincent of Beauvais, in a lavishly appointed study in which several volumes of similarly huge proportions to Edward's own manuscript are on display. A small mirror on the table before him alludes to the mirror of history and experience provided by his text (see also nos. 17 and 21).

Jean de Vignay, *Miroir historial*, Vol. 1 (French translation of Vincent of Beauvais, *Speculum historiale*)
Bruges, *c.* 1479–80
470 x 340 mm
British Library, Royal 14 E. i, vol. 1, f. 3

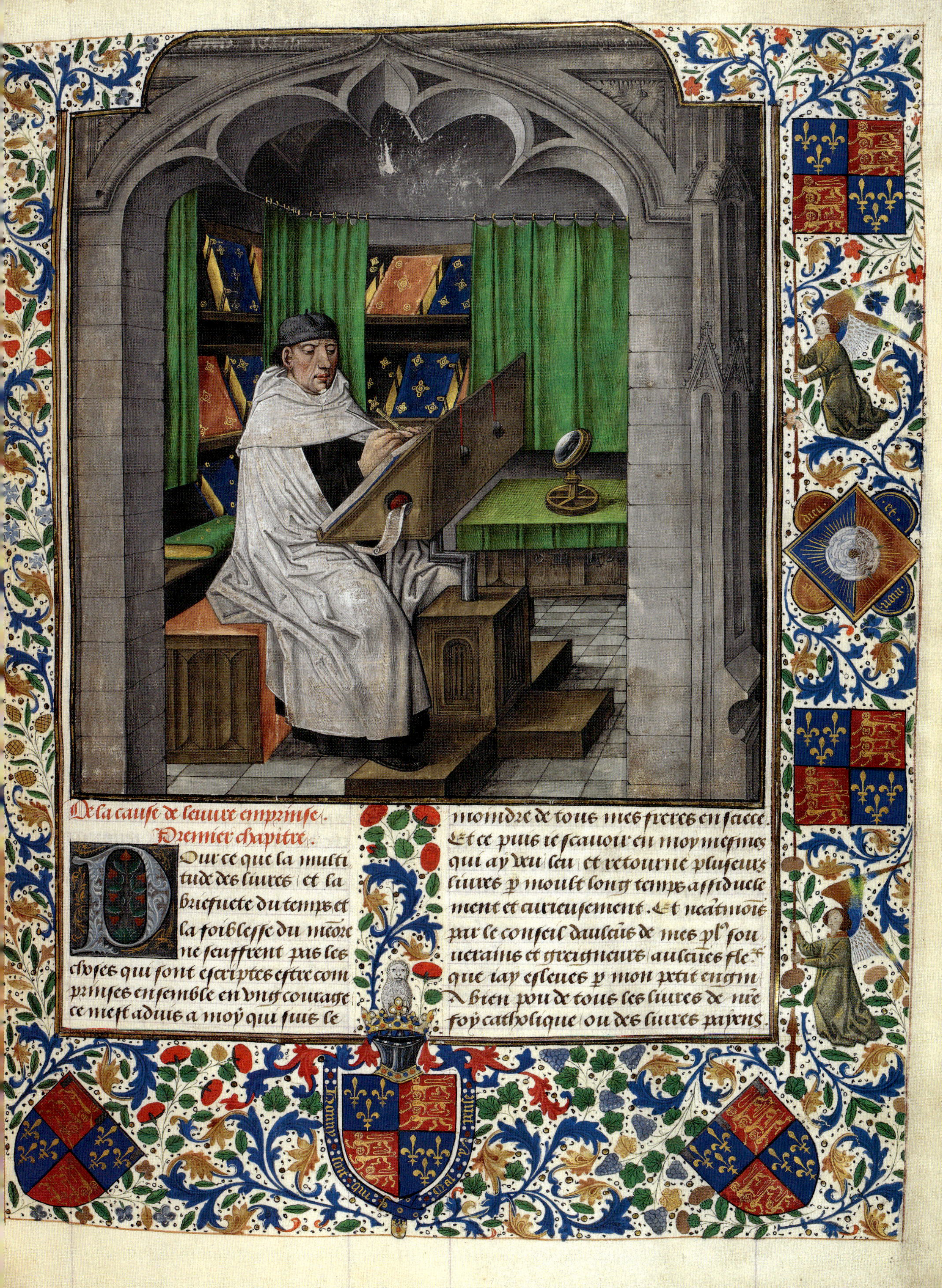

Pour ce que la multitude des liures, et la briefuete du temps et la foiblesse du memore ne seuffrent pas les choses qui sont escriptes estre comprinses ensemble en vnit courage, ce mest aduis a moy qui suis le moindre de tous mes freres en saece. Et ce puis ie scauoir en moy mesmes qui ay veu leu, et retourne plusieurs liures p moult lonc temps assiduelement et curieusement. Et neatmoie par le conseil daulcais de mes pl' souuerains et greigneurs aulcaies fle que iay esleues p mon petit engin A bien pou de tous les liures de nre foy catholique ou des liures payens.

34 Charles of Orleans in the Tower of London

This extraordinary image is justly famous as the earliest-known topographically accurate depiction of London. It accompanies verses *Des Nouvelles d'Albyon* (*News from England*) in a large and elaborate collection of the poems of Charles, Duke of Orleans (d. 1465). Charles had been captured at the battle of Agincourt (1415), and spent the next twenty-five years in England (part of the time imprisoned in the Tower of London), during which time he composed these poems. The Tower is visible prominently in the foreground of the image, and within the Tower the author is seen writing, perhaps this work, or perhaps the poem copied on this page, addressed to his cousin Philip the Good, Duke of Burgundy (r. 1419–67), who ultimately paid Charles's ransom.

Charles's poems were disseminated widely. This lavish copy includes a selection of 166 of his verses about politics or romance; these themes are reflected also in the other texts included in the volume. The presence in the book of the arms of England supported by Edward IV's lions of March and other emblems, such as the Yorkist white rose in splendour, suggest that this was another of the large-scale manuscripts intended for Edward IV (r. 1461–83). Interestingly, however, this manuscript is the only one that is not a work of history (compare nos. 30–33). The book was apparently unfinished at Edward's death, but the text, or perhaps the completed images, were of sufficient interest that the rest of the decoration was completed for Henry VII: his arms were added to the border around the first large image.

Charles of Orléans, Poems; with other Texts relating to Love and Princely Instruction
Bruges, *c.* 1483 (this image) with later additions, *c.* 1492–*c.* 1500
370 x 260 mm
British Library, Royal 16 F. ii, f. 73

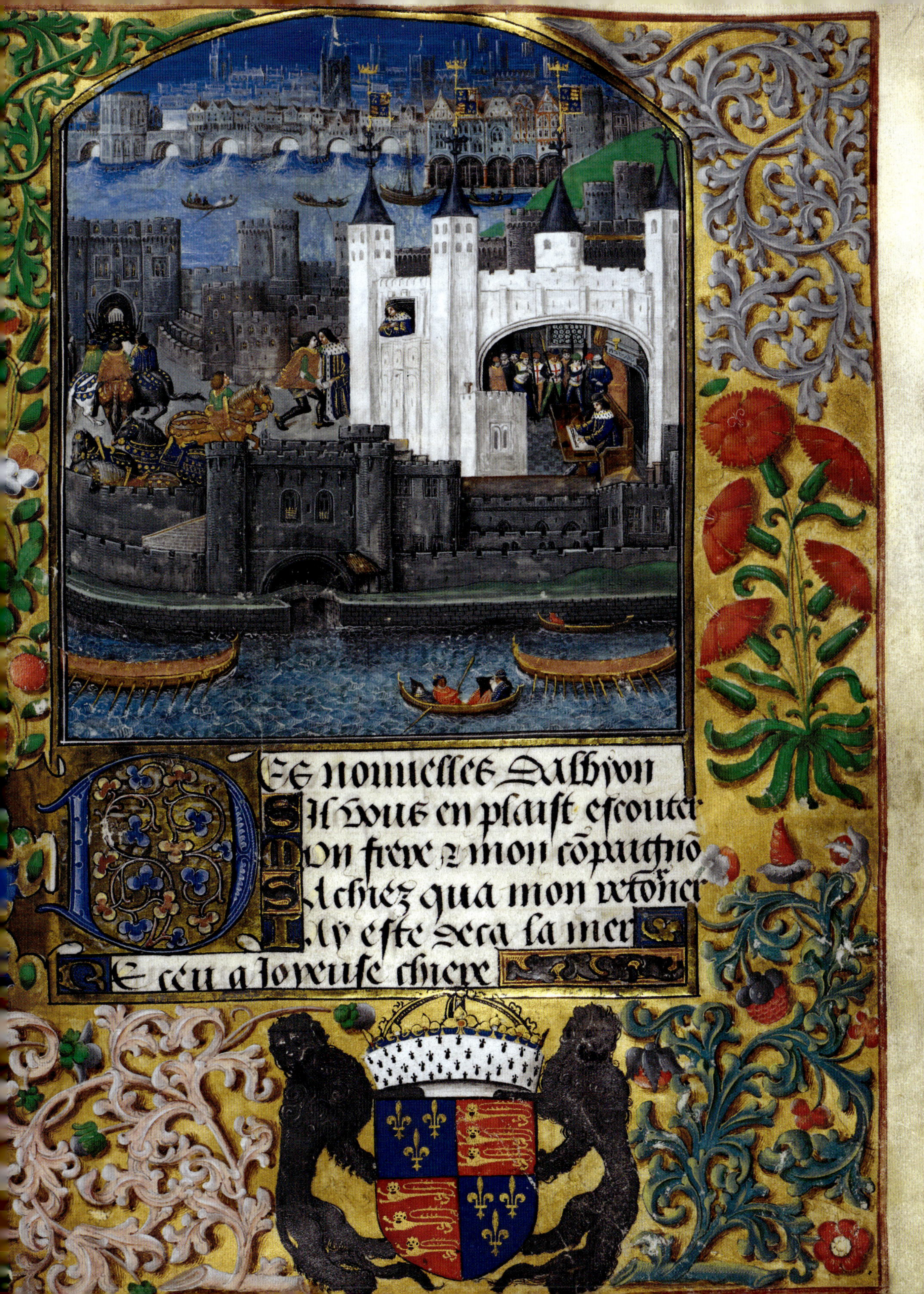

Les nouuelles dalbyon
Sil vous en plaust escouter
Mon frere & mon compaignon
Sachez qua mon retourner
Ay este dela la mer
Receu a ioyeuse chiere

35 Henry VII and his courtiers discussing a book of astrology

The treatises in this volume are all astrological in content, and include some that feature political prophecies as well as astronomical and planetary tables. That the compilation was intended for a king, probably Henry VII, is clear from the fact that several initials include the red Lancastrian rose appropriate to Henry's ancestry, as well as the red-and-white Tudor rose reflecting the union with the Yorkists effected by Henry's marriage to Elizabeth of York, the daughter of Edward IV. In addition, the Tudor livery colours of green and white are featured as the background to some of the constellations, such as the Dragon, shown as the red dragon that formed one of the heraldic supporters of Henry's royal arms (see no. 36).

The King is also pictured in an initial at the beginning of the treatise 'On the Revolutions of the Year of the World' in one of the texts, the *Liber Astronomiae*. Here Henry is surrounded by members of his court, including one standing directly behind the King, probably the Lord Great Chamberlain, who holds a sword and wears a so-called 'collar of SSes' or 'Esses', a livery collar and former Lancastrian badge. The King shows a book to a French ambassador who displays a shield with fleurs-de-lis as authentication of his mission. That such a book would have been welcomed by the King is likely, given his interest in astrology and the specific prophecies concerning him that were contained within it. Whether or not he ever received the book is unclear, but it later passed into the Duke of Norfolk's collection and was purchased for the nation in 1831.

Collection of Astrological Treatises
England, 1490
440 x 300 mm
British Library, Arundel 66, f. 201 (detail)

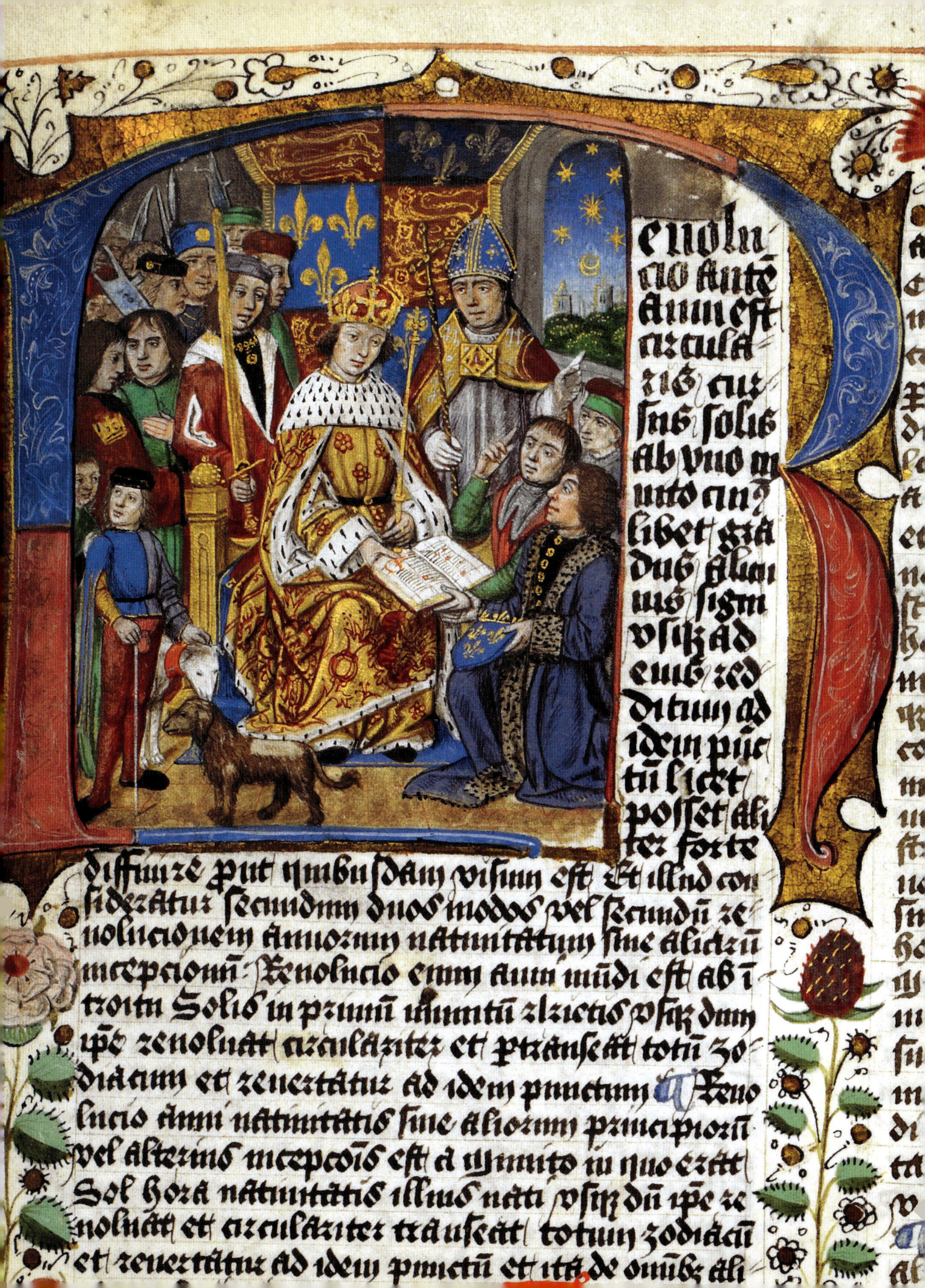

Reuolu-
cio Ante
Anni est
circula-
cionis cur
sus solis
ab uno pu-
ncto cui-
libet gra-
dus alicui-
us signi
usque ad
eius redi-
tum ad
idem pun-
cti licet
posset ali-
ter forte

diffinire prout quibusdam visum est. Et illud con-
sideratur secundum duos modos vel secundum re-
uolucionem annorum natiuitatum siue aliarum
inceptionum. Reuolucio enim anni mundi est ab in-
troitu Solis in primum minutum arietis usque dum
ipse reuoluat circulariter et pertranseat totum zodiacum et reuertatur ad idem punctum. Reuolucio anni natiuitatis siue aliorum principiorum
vel alterius inceptionis est ab eo minuto in quo erat
Sol hora natiuitatis illius nati usque dum ipse reuoluat et circulariter transeat totum zodiacum
et reuertatur ad idem punctum et ita de omnibus ali[is]

36 Henry VII presenting the Indenture

Very few medieval or Tudor bindings survive; the one covering this book is a particularly impressive example (pictured below). It is a 'chemise' binding or cloth cover in red velvet lined with damask that may have been imported from Italy. This chemise wrapper covers four indentures, or series of agreements, between Henry VII and the monks of Westminster Abbey, dated 1504. Two copies of the indenture were made and, remarkably, both survive with their original bindings – this one and the other now in the National Archives. Attached to the covers of both are a series of bosses in silver gilt and enamel, decorated with the King's emblems. Five original wax seals with impressions of the King also survive with the present copy; these are affixed to the documents and authenticate the covenants contained within them. The upper edges of the pages and wooden covers are cut in curved lines, consistent with more typical indentures on parchment sheets that were cut apart so that they could be fitted back together upon redemption or to verify the authenticity of claimed contractual obligations.

The grandeur of these indentures is also demonstrated by the fact that each begins with an illustration and a painted border. Here the border is decorated with the Beaufort portcullises of Henry's mother, Margaret Beaufort (for her prayerbook see no. 22), and his arms, held by his supporters, a dragon and a white hound. In the initial Henry hands the indenture to John Islip (b. 1464, d. 1532), the abbot of Westminster, who with his monks kneels before him.

Quadripartite Indenture
London, 1504
370 x 255 mm
British Library, Harley 1498, f. 1

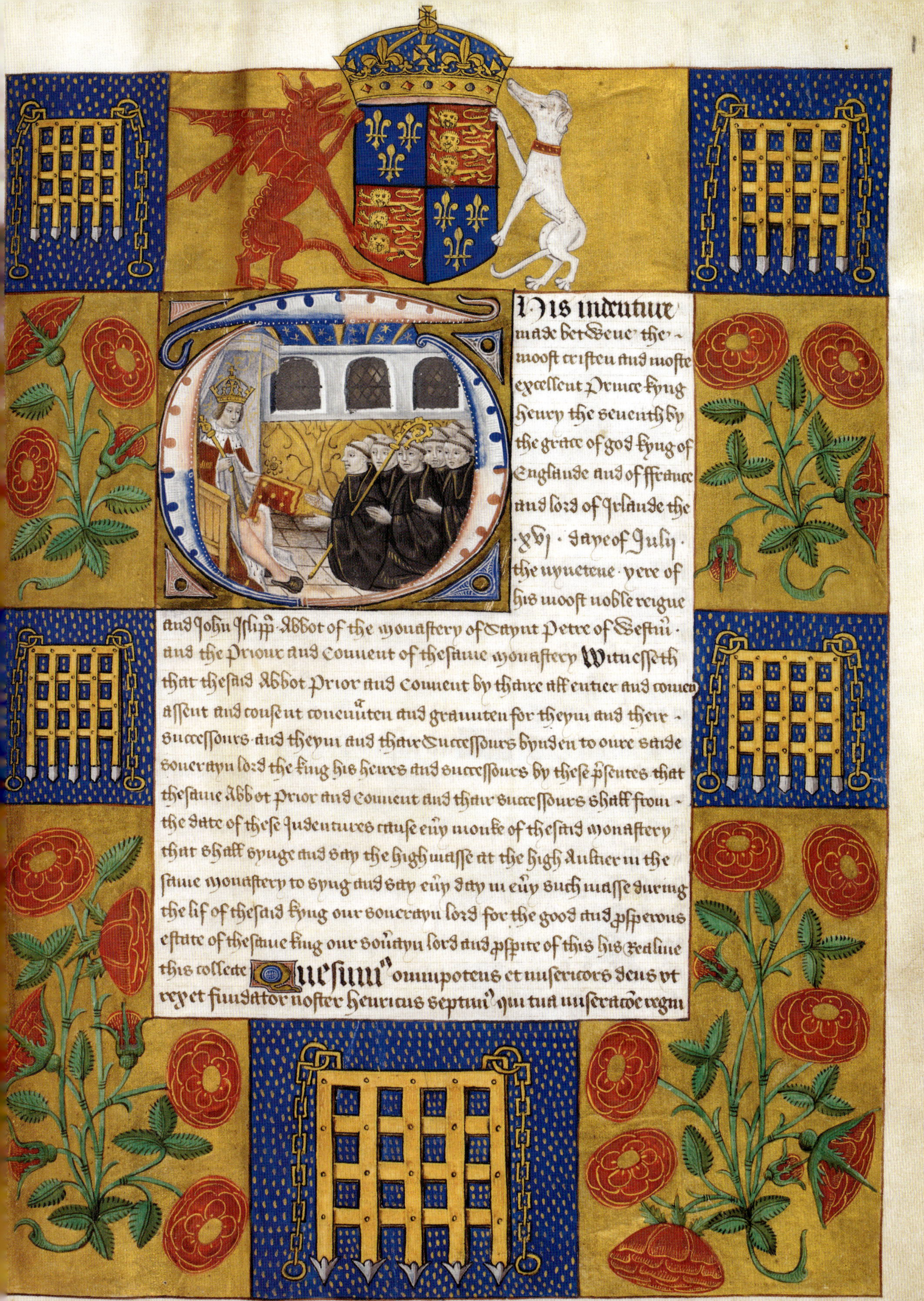

THis indenture made betwene the moost cristen and moste excellent Prince kyng Henry the seuenth by the grace of god kyng of Englande and of ffraunce and lord of Irlande the xvj . daye of July . the nyntene . yere of his moost noble reigne and John Islipp Abbot of the monastery of Saynt Petre of Westm̄ and the Priour and Couuent of the same monastery Witnesseth that the said Abbot Prior and Couuent by theire aff entier and comen assent and consent conuenten and graunten for theym and their successours and theym and their Successours bynden to oure saide soueraȳn lord the king his heires and successours by these presentes that the same Abbot Prior and Couuent and their successours shall from the date of these Indentures cause euy monke of the said monastery that shall synge and say the high masse at the high Aulter in the same monastery to syng and say euy day in euy such masse during the lif of the said kyng our soueraȳn lord for the good and prosperous estate of the same king our soueraȳn lord and prosperite of this his Realme this collecte Quesuȳ omnipotens et misericors deus vt rex et fundator noster henricus septim̄ qui tua miseracōe regni

37 The translator presenting the manuscript to Henry VII

Henry VII's new palace at Richmond had a library filled with 'many goodly pleasaunt bokes of werkes full delitfull, sage, mery, and also right cunnyng'. This French book was probably one of them. The volume was a gift to Henry from the French ambassador and translator of the book, Claude de Seyssel. The principal opening features arms of England and an image of Henry VII enthroned, with the royal motto *Dieu Est* [sic] *Mon Droit*. Its preface includes further evidence about the King's library, which is otherwise sadly lacking in documentation. According to de Seyssel, he found the King's library to be 'very fine and very well appointed' ('tres belle et tres bien acoustree').

The text of the work was designed to appeal to Henry's interests. De Seyssel explained that he had heard that Henry was 'was well entertained in reading and hearing history and other topics appropriate for a noble and wise prince'. This stirring story of the military expedition (*Anabasis*, or 'going up') of the Persian Cyrus the Younger (d. 401 BC), as told by one of its key participants Xenophon, was doubtless calculated to be one of these histories that would be both well received and entertaining for the King. Like the histories ordered by Edward IV, Henry's father-in-law, this copy is illustrated with large paintings, which presumably would have formed part of the entertainment of the book.

Xenophon, *Anabasis*, (French translation by Claude de Seyssel)
Bourges, *c.* 1506
320 x 225 mm
British Library, Royal 19 C. vi, f. 17

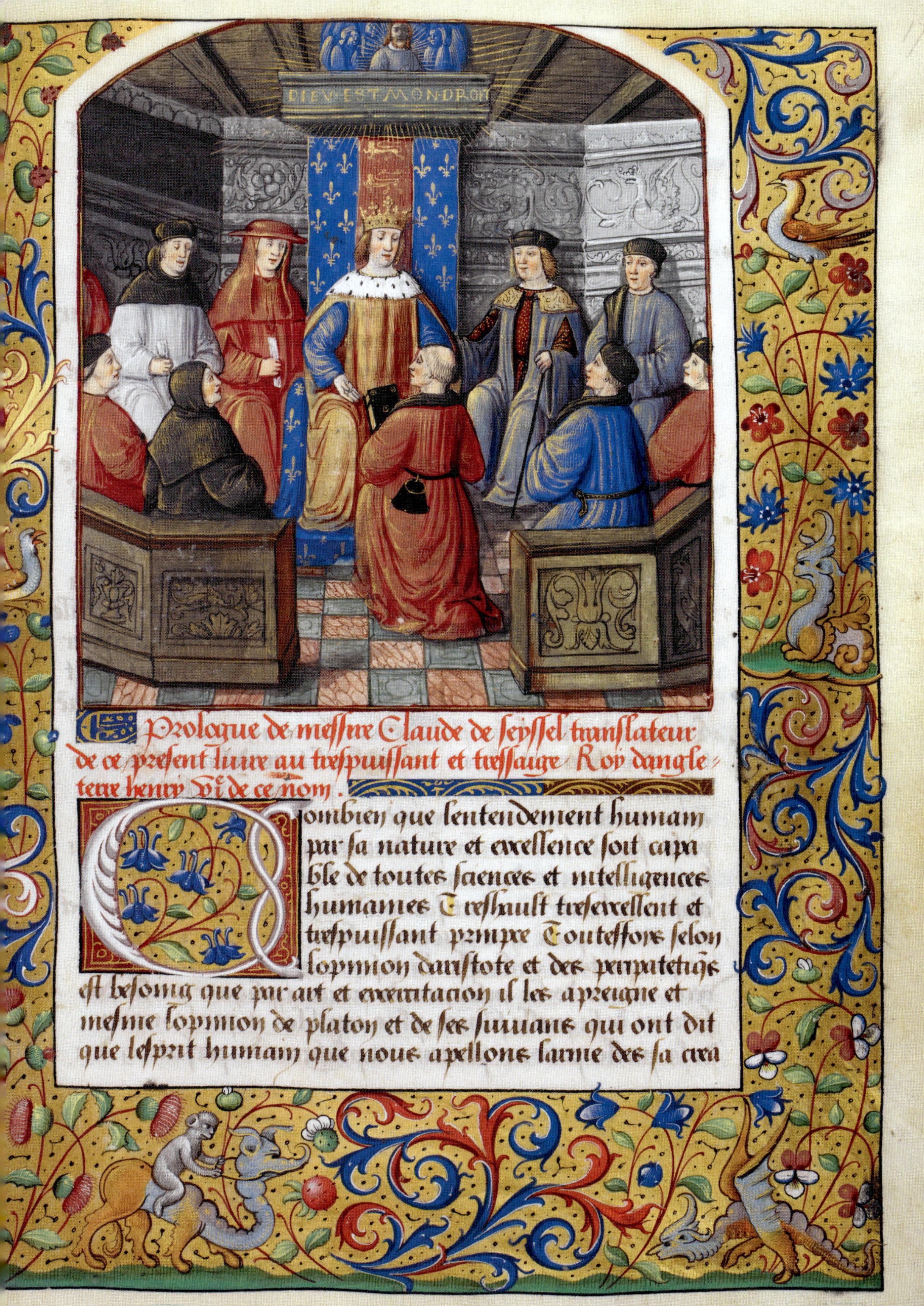

Prologue de messire Claude de seyssel translateur
de ce present liure au trespuissant et tressaige Roy dangle
terre henry vi de ce nom.

Combien que lentendement humain
par sa nature et excellence soit capa
ble de toutes sciences et intelligences
humaines Treshault tresexcellent et
trespuissant prince Touteffois selon
lopinion daristote et des peripatetiqs
est besoing que par art et exercitacion il les apreigne et
mesme lopinion de platon et de ses suiuans qui ont dit
que lesprit humain que nous apellons larme des sa crea

38 The author and the arms of Henry VIII

This opulent humanistic manuscript is one of the few Italian illuminated manuscripts in the Old Royal library. It is a copy of a Latin translation of a Greek text by Lucian of Samosata (b. *c.* 120, d. *c.* 180) popularised by Italian humanists at the beginning of the fifteenth century, that accompanies a series of fables drawing on Aesop by Pandolfo Collenuccio of Pesaro (b. 1444, d. 1504). Collenuccio was in the service of both the Sforza and the Medici families, before being executed as a traitor by Lorenzo de' Medici (b. 1449, d. 1492). The decoration at the beginning of the text makes it clear that the book was written as a gift for Henry VIII, because it includes his arms surrounded by the Garter in the lower border. The donor was Henry's Surveyor-General, Geoffrey Chamber. During a visit to Italy in the early part of the sixteenth century Chamber commissioned a scribe of the papal chancery to write the work, and the artist Attavante degli Attavanti of Florence (b. 1452, d. *c.* 1520–25) to paint the portrait of the author and the elaborate border.

The manuscript has an interesting later history as well. After its presentation to Henry VIII (r. 1509–47) it left the Old Royal library and came into the possession of the President of Magdalen College, Oxford, Nicholas Bond (b. 1540, d. 1608). Bond subsequently presented it to James I's son Henry Frederick, Prince of Wales (b. 1594, d. 1612) on the Prince's graduation from Magdalen in 1605. Like Henry VIII, Prince Henry Frederick was one of the four main contributors of illuminated manuscripts to the Old Royal library through his acquisition of the library of John Lumley (b. *c.* 1533, d. 1609), 1st Baron Lumley. The Prince's large collection of books and manuscripts were transferred from his personal library at St James's Palace to the Old Royal library on the Prince's untimely death, probably from typhoid, at the age of eighteen.

Pandolfo Collenuccio, *Apologues*, and Lucian of Samosata, *Dialogues*
Rome and Florence, *c.* 1509–17
320 x 225 mm
British Library, Royal 12 C. viii, f. 4

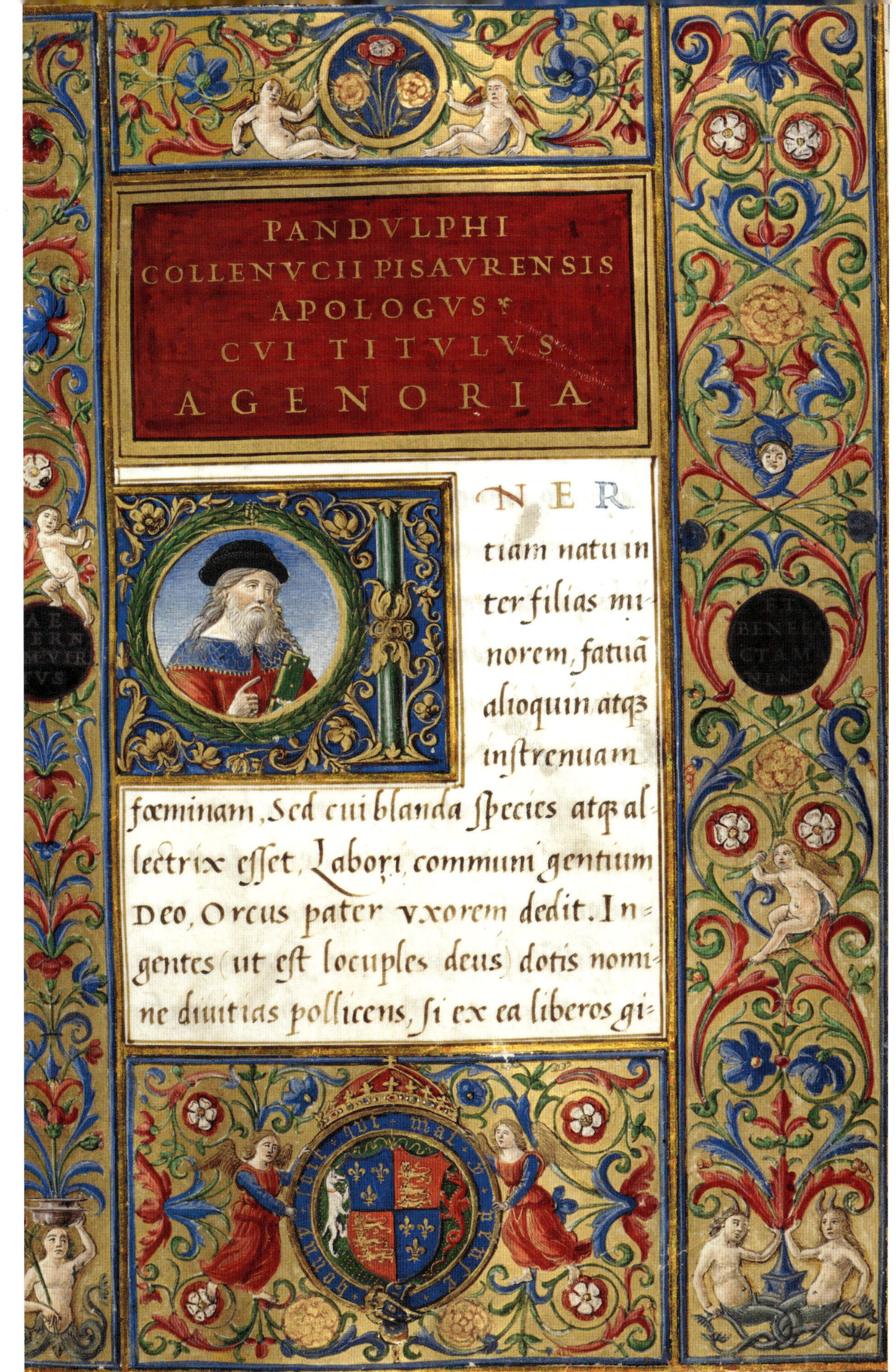

N E R
tiam natu in
ter filias mi
norem, fatuã
alioquin atqz
instrenuam
fœminam, Sed cui blanda species atqz al
lectrix esset, Labori, communi gentium
Deo, Orcus pater vxorem dedit. In=
gentes (ut est locuples deus) dotis nomi=
ne diuitias pollicens, si ex ea liberos gi

39 The crowned Tudor rose

Many of the royal manuscripts highlighted in this book were highly personalised
for their intended royal owners. Perhaps this is one of the reasons that
individualised illuminated manuscripts – for those who could afford them –
continued to be made well after the advent of printing. This large and grand
choirbook produced for Henry VIII (r. 1509–47) near the beginning of his reign
is a good example. Its first page (pictured) is covered with allegorical and symbolic
imagery unique to Henry.

Dominating the top centre of the page is a crowned Tudor rose of red and white.
Through their marriage Henry's parents had joined together the Lancastrian red
and the York white roses: Henry VII's mother, Margaret Beaufort (d. 1509), was
a descendant of John of Gaunt, Duke of Lancaster (b. 1340, d. 1399), and Henry
VII's wife was Elizabeth of York (d. 1503). The poem below this expresses the
virtues of the two roses, finally united in Henry. Below is the garden of England,
guarded by Henry's supporters, the red dragon and the white greyhound, and
in which Catherine of Aragon's pomegranate tree is planted (to the right).
At the root of the tree are the symbols of Henry's two sisters Margaret and
Mary, represented by a daisy (or marguerite), to the left, and by a yellow
marigold, to the right.

The music that followed the allegorical poem was no less special. It includes
two motets composed expressly for the King and another four that addressed
issues of concern to him. Henry was himself a musician, and the finest musicians
of the time were gathered at his court. This elegant manuscript demonstrates
that amongst Henry's collections were impressive and highly personalised
musical scores.

Motets for Henry VIII
Southern Netherlands (Antwerp?), 1516
490 x 355 mm
British Library, Royal 11 E. xi, f. 2

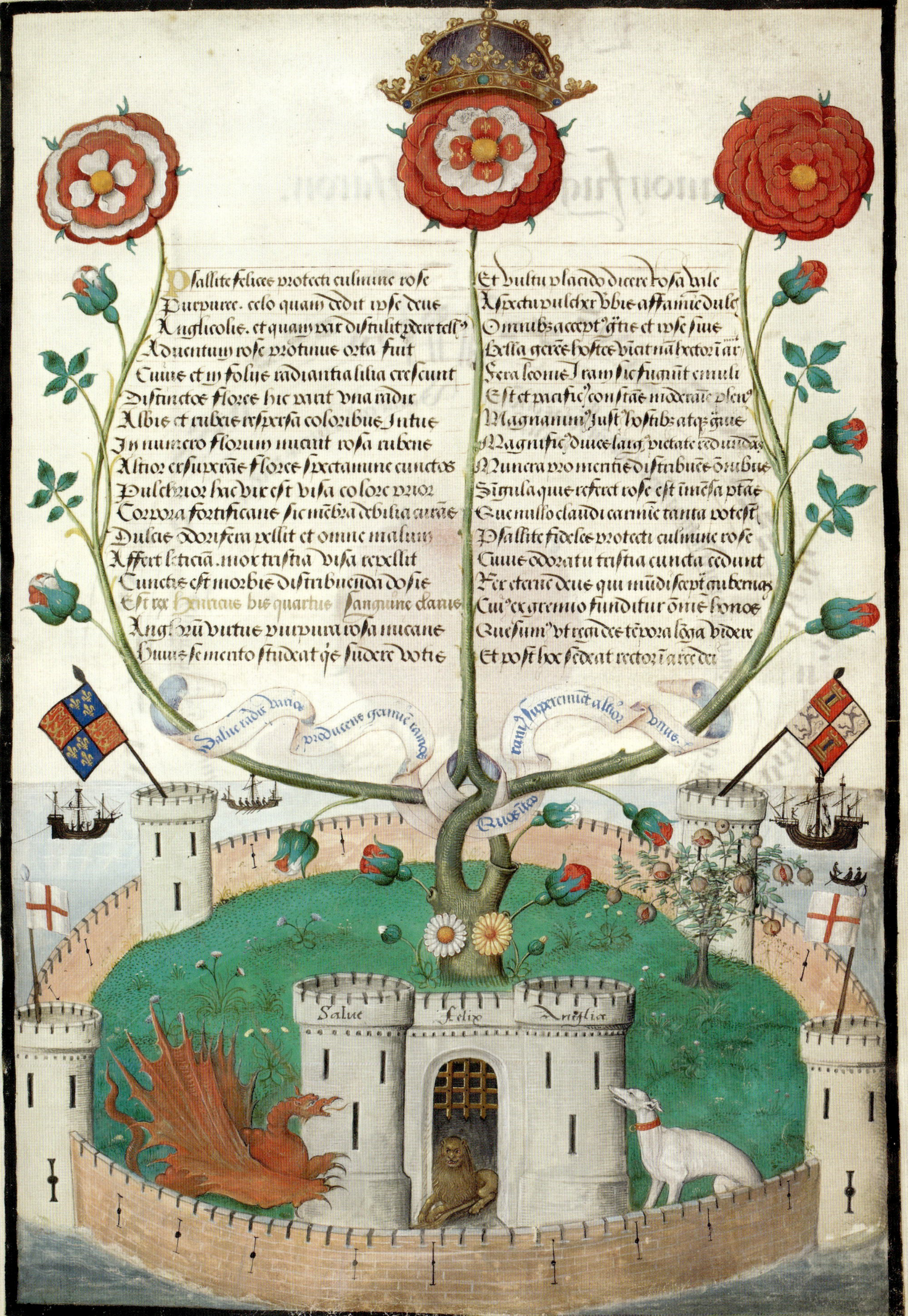

Psallite felices protecti culmine rose
Purpuree. celo quam dedit ipse deus
Anglicolis. et quam dat distulit preter tell
Adventum rose protinus orta fuit
Cuius et in foliis radiantia lilia crescunt
Distinctos flores hic uarit una indir
Albis et rubeis respersa coloribus Intuis
In numero florum micant rosa rubens
Altior et supreme flores spectamine cunctos
Pulchrior hic uir est uisa colore prior
Corpora fortificans sic membra debilia curans
Dulcis odorifera pellit et omne malum
Affert leticiam. mor tristia uisa repellit
Cunctis est morbis distribuenda dosis
Est rex Henricus bis quartus sanguine clarus
Angl rum uirtus purpura rosa micans
Huius se mento studeat qui sudere uotis

Et uultu placido dicere rosa uale
Aspectu pulcher ubis affamie dulc
Omnibus acceptus este et ipse suis
Bella gerens hostes uicat na hector i ar
Fera leonis Iram sic fugiunt emuli
Est et prasic constae moderate plen
Magnanimus Just hostibus atque ue
Magnific duces larg pietate redundas
Munera pro mentie distribuis oribus
Singula que refert rose est inmensa ptae
Sue nullo claudi carnie tanta potest
Psallite fideles protecti culmine rose
Cuius odoratu tristia cuncta cedunt
Fer etenic deus qui mundi septa gubernas
Cui ex gremio funditur omnis honor
Quesum ut regi dei tempora longa uidere
Et post hoc sedeat rector in arce dei

Salue radix danq producens germi ram
ram supereminet altior bonus
Quesitio

Salue
Felix
Anglia

40 A royal binding

Despite the riches of the Old Royal library, textually and artistically, very few original bindings remain in the collection. In part, this may result from a fire in 1731 at Ashburnham House, Little Dean's Yard. Now part of Westminster School, this site was then occupied by the Old Royal library. During the fire these volumes were reportedly thrown out of the second-storey window to save them from being burnt. As a result, this remarkable binding with the arms of Henry VIII ornamented with gold thread and seed pearls is a precious survival.

The book contained within the embroidered binding is a description in French of the Holy Land. Interestingly, the author presented this very text to Henry's rival Francis I (r. 1515–47) as well (and indeed a Latin copy to the Pope), and the books of the two great monarchs are strikingly similar in layout. De Brion personalised the copies with an individualised preface to each king; the decoration was specific to each as well, with Tudor roses and French fleurs-de-lis.

In the post-mortem inventory of Henry's possessions this book was described as being 'covered with vellat enbrawdred'. From the inventory it is clear that the King owned many such elaborate bindings in velvet or in leather of various colours, often ornamented further with precious stones. This rare example (another is the much-worn velvet cover of his Psalter (no. 41), is an important record of the way in which valuable royal illuminated manuscripts were made even grander.

Martin de Brion, *Tresample Description de Toute la Terre Saincte*
Paris (?), *c.* 1540
230 x 160 mm
British Library, Royal 20 A. iv, upper cover

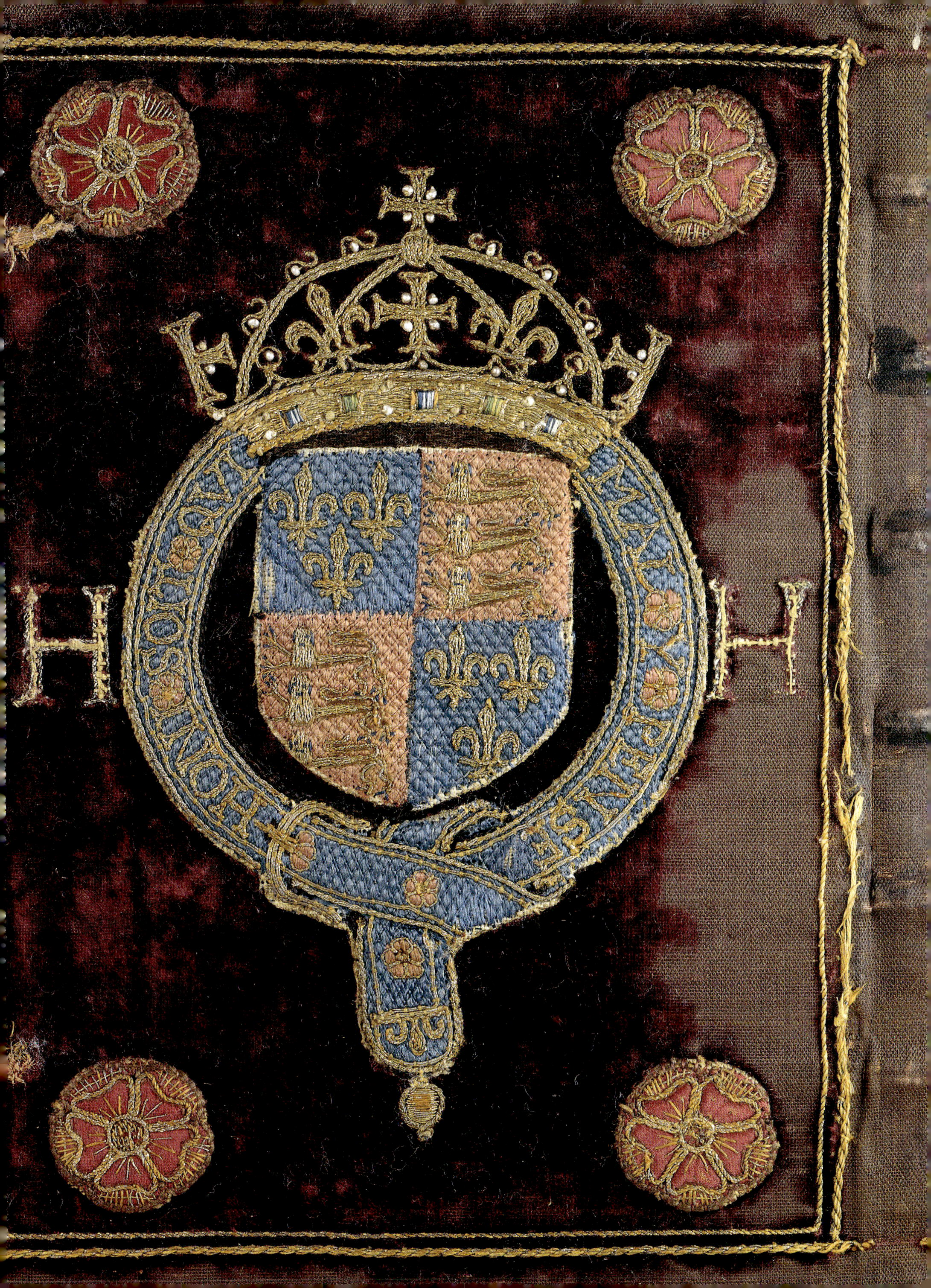
HONI SOIT QVI MALY PENSE

41 Henry VIII as King David

The illustrations that Henry VIII commissioned in a Psalter for his own use in around 1540 demonstrate that he saw himself as a king in the tradition of the biblical King David. In the Psalter's opening portrait of Henry seated in a chair in his bedchamber holding an open book, the King looks out at the viewer, who was initially Henry himself. Henry was forty-nine when the book was made, and in this image he looks his age. It is not too fanciful to see the open book that the King holds as a representation of this very Psalter, the red velvet binding of which still survives, albeit in a rather worn state. This portrait occurs at Psalm 1, the location in a Psalter where an image of David was traditional (compare nos. 5 and 8).

The King commissioned the Psalter from Jean Mallard, who wrote out the Psalms in a beautifully clear humanistic script and signed his name in the dedicatory preface as the King's poet. Mallard may have painted this portrait and the three others in the book that also feature Henry as David, once with Goliath (Psalm 26), another with David's harp (Psalm 52), and another in prayer (Psalm 68). By this date a manuscript Psalter in Latin rather than the more popular Book of Hours was an unusual choice. Perhaps the opportunity presented for a direct alignment between the King and David accounts, in part, for the commissioning of such a personalised copy of the text. That the King used the book is clear from extensive Latin annotations in his own hand, including the marginal note reproduced here to 'Note who is blessed' (N[ota] quis sit beat[us]).

The Henry VIII Psalter
London, *c.* 1540
205 x 140 mm
British Library, Royal 2 A. xvi, f. 3

Beatus vir qui non abiit in consilio impiorum, & in via peccatorum non stetit, & in cathedra pestilentiæ non sedit.

The Royal Manuscripts project is supported by

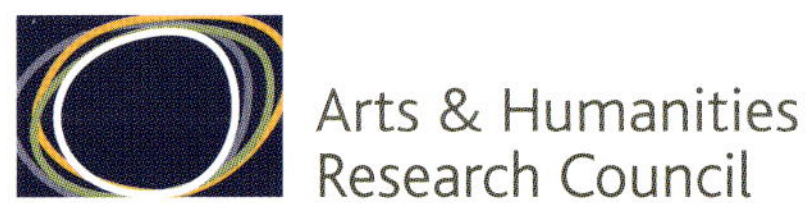

First published in 2011 by
The British Library
96 Euston Road
London NW1 2DB

On the occasion of the exhibition at the British Library
'Royal Manuscripts: The Genius of Illumination'
11 November 2011 – 13 March 2012

British Library Cataloguing in Publication Data
A catalogue record for this publication is available from the British Library

ISBN 978 0 7123 5855 2

Designed and typeset by Kate Bates, British Library Design Office
Colour reproduction by Dot Gradations Ltd, Essex
Printed in Hong Kong by Great Wall Printing Co. Ltd